FULL ON THE EYE

Perspectives on the World, the Church
and the Faith

Bill Clinkenbeard and Ian Gilmour

The Bavelaw Press

The Authors

Ian Gilmour was brought up with his two brothers at Millerston, near Glasgow. He was educated at Clifton High School, Glasgow College of Commerce and Glasgow College of Technology, before graduating B.D. from Glasgow University. A member of St George's and St Peter's Church in Easterhouse, he became assistant minister at Garthamloch and Craigend East in 1984. The following year he was received as the fifth minister to serve at Drylaw Parish Church in Edinburgh. Drylaw is a mixed housing area having 6,500 residents, most of the area consisting of council housing built in the 1950's. Ian's wife Donna is a nurse, and they have two teenage daughters. He enjoys most sports, including swimming, rugby and golf, which he plays regularly but 'erratically'.

Bill Clinkenbeard was born and raised in Lincoln, Nebraska in the United States. After graduating from the University of Nebraska in electronic engineering, he worked for Convair Astronautics. He received his B.D. from McCormick Theological Seminary in Chicago in 1964. After postgraduate study at Glasgow University and Yale Divinity School, he received the S.T.M. degree from Yale in 1966. He served for three years as minister of Wood River Parish Church in Nebraska before returning to Scotland for further postgraduate study. He has been minister of Carrick Knowe Parish Church in Edinburgh since 1971 and recently served as Moderator of Edinburgh Presbytery. He is married to a Scot, Janette, who is a G.P. and they have three grown-up children. His golf is in equilibrium.

To Mum, Donna, Jennifer and Gillian,
with thanks to Cliff and Morag for many stimulating
conversations

To Janette,
Bob and Esther

Acknowledgements

The trouble with writing and publishing a book is that in the end it assumes such an awesome and final form. This is not how we would wish it to be. The point has always been to *begin* a significant discussion about the church, the faith, and the world rather than to *end* it. The finality of the printed page makes us more than ever aware of the deficiencies of this work. It would have been helpful to have had more time, but time is of the very essence of the problem. Too many issues need to be dealt with *now*.

We are grateful to many people for help in the preparation of this book. They have made many useful suggestions and criticisms from which we have learned much. Any shortcomings, however, must be attributed only to us and not to them. Thanks are due to Ian Brady, Graeme and Sybil Brown, Ron Ferguson, Iain Matheson, Barbara MacHaffie, George McCaskill, and Neil Ross for reading the manuscript and making valuable suggestions, to Alison Brown for the cover design, and to Ann Thom for advice about printing. We are grateful to our wives Donna and Janette for their support, criticism, and tolerance. Finally, we are grateful for a multitude of unnamed people who over the years have provided us with such rich experience in the ministry.

October 1994, Balerno

Afterwards I will pour out my spirit on everyone:
your sons and daughters will proclaim my message;
your old men will have dreams, and your young
                         men will see visions.-- Joel

It is not possible to have a living church with dead
members, no matter how well organised and ably led.
                         --Joseph Haroutunian

The aspect of things that are most important for us
are hidden because of their simplicity and familiarity.
                         --Ludwig Wittgenstein

Contents

Introduction   2

Perspectives on the World   6

Chapter 1 "The Blind Leading the Blind"   7

Chapter 2 "The Gaze of the One-Eyed God"   20

Chapter 3 "Fatal Attractions"   31

Perspectives on the Church   40

Chapter 4 "Womb without a View"   41

Chapter 5 "Clock Without Hands"   49

Chapter 6 "A Narrowing Panorama"   58

Perspectives on the Faith   67

Chapter 7 "On a Clear Day..."   68

Chapter 8 "An Alternative Vista"   75

Chapter 9 "Full on the Eye"   91

Notes   103

INTRODUCTION

The purpose of this book is suitably simple and modest: to provide a critique of the world and the church from the perspective of the Christian faith! You may well ask how anyone can be either audacious enough or foolish enough to make such an attempt. The answer is that it seems necessary because an ominous silence seems to have settled over the church these days. Very few seem prepared to 'nail their colours to the mast' by developing any public view about the flux of the world and the state of the church in relation to the Christian faith.

We are not so much anxious to prop up an ancient institution as we are concerned about the 'tail-spin' our society now appears to be entering. We want to look at certain current trends in the world and remind readers that the church still has something to say about the world: namely, about the short-sightedness which afflicts it at the end of the twentieth century. Hopefully the church, having learned something from its many and frequent failures (clericalism, abuse of power, persecution of some minorities), has something to teach the world from its successes (stability and order, accumulated wisdom, care for other minorities).

Long ago, Walter Lippman wrote: "Whirl is king, having driven out Zeus." That observation is more than ever true today. The texture of ordinary life seems to be changing at an ever increasing rate, leaving people rather dazed and breathless. The news daily portrays a world regularly convulsed, agitated or deranged. It is not easy for people to come to grips with such rapid change. Does the church have any stability to offer, any coherent and unifying vision which would help to make sense of the world? We are convinced that it does.

We have written this work with the 'thinking person' in mind. This does not mean the 'intellectual', but rather the person who reflects regularly on his or her experience in the world. He or she may be in or out of the church, think of himself or herself as Christian or not, be religious or irreligious. It seemed to us that a fresh, straightforward, realistic, and occasionally even humorous look at the world, the church, and the faith would not be likely to damage anyone's health and might even do some good!

We write as parish ministers in the Church of Scotland, having experience in both Scotland and the United States. Between us we have spent over thirty years on the church's 'front-line'. The parish minister is one of a decreasing number of professional people who are readily accessible today. Our reflection and writing has been done in those little compressed spaces which appear between funerals, weddings, and a multiplicity of meetings, when the problems of how to organise worship on Sunday or find new youth leaders were also exercising the mind. So this does not purport to be an academic work. We have not had the time (or possibly the sense!) to read the latest scholarly material about what parish ministers are doing, or haven't done, or should be doing. For the most part, this work reflects our regular contact with ordinary people who live in the real world and have to try to figure it out, whether they are inside or outside the church. Our starting point is experience rather than revelation, although we believe that our experience is informed by revelation. At its simplest, this book is a statement: This is how it looks to us from where we are.

We have organised our reflection around the theme of 'vision'. Like other themes or metaphors, this has its advantages and disadvantages. H. Richard Neibuhr suggested that it was always important to consider what metaphors people were using to see how that usage shaped and limited their work. Whatever the limitations of 'vision', we hope that the reader will discover some new ways of looking at things.

Some Christians might be disturbed by some of our critical comments about the church in Part II, but it seemed important to be honest about the church and the faith. Mere contentment with established practices in the church too often masquerades as loyal discipleship. In Part I, inevitably, we have had to be selective in our analysis of trends in the world. Trying to get a critical grasp of the world today is like trying to put socks onto an octopus.

It is always much easier to be negative than it is to be positive. For this reason we have tried in Part III to make a positive affirmation about those patterns we would like to see emerge for

4

faith and the church in the future. We have no doubt that these patterns may be found to be incomplete or flawed. Our intention is simply to encourage a useful and effective debate about the faith, the church, and the world. To further this aim we have included some questions for discussion at the end of each chapter in the hope that this might facilitate group study.

We have worked at trying to keep the language simple, for we do not accept the proposition that profound ideas require abstract or obtuse language for expression. We believe that many academics (even theologians) may unwittingly confuse their readers and even deceive themselves by using such jargon.

**Well-known theologians
and other academics,
dwell securely in a world
comprised by their polemics.**

Therefore, the task we have undertaken is an old but ever - essential one: to look at the direction in which society is moving, then to encourage the church to spend itself in order to further the formation of a healthier, more just society in the future. In consequence the church may recover its self-respect and sense of purpose as its focus turns outward upon the world rather than inward upon its own workings.

Part I

Perspectives on the World

Chapter 1

THE BLIND LEADING THE BLIND

If a blind man leads a blind man, both will fall into a pit
-- Jesus of Nazareth

It belongs largely to the genius of the western world to have brought into being a new reality: individualism. This is not to say that this new reality is a very recent discovery. The individualism of the West has long been recognised and dissected by scholars, but like other human patterns which through time become woven into the fabric of life, it is simply taken for granted by most of us. We assume that this is the way society has always been organised and ought to be organised. Indeed, in the United Kingdom recent governments have encouraged the reign of individualism by promoting 'individual freedom' and 'individual rights'. Margaret Thatcher placed just such a stress when she addressed the 1988 General Assembly of the Church of Scotland as Prime Minister:

What is certain, however, is that any set of social and economic arrangements which is not founded on the acceptance of

7

individual responsibility will do nothing but harm. We are all responsible for our own actions.[1]

In Lady Thatcher's view the individual is the fundamental unit or building block in the social structure; his or her 'acceptance of responsibility' is the foundation stone for society. This means that the social order is merely a collection of individuals, and its character is determined by their will. Society is thus a one-way street. The formation of a good society depends upon responsible individuals, but the formation of responsible individuals does not depend upon being in a good society. Building a good social structure demands good personal building blocks, but where and how such blocks are made is not clear.

There is however, another and quite different viewpoint which is accepted by many students of society. Peter Berger, for example, can write: "Society not only controls our movements, but shapes our identity, our thought and our emotions. The structures of society become the structures of our own consciousness."[2] From this perspective, society is seen as a natural entity in and of itself, within which individuals are born, learn, grow and develop. The language, customs, and patterns of social life precede any individual and provide the necessary conditions for individual freedom and responsibility. Man is not simply in society, but society is in man. The promoted view that society is merely a collection of individuals is symptomatic of a peculiar and dangerous kind of blindness which is pervasive and influential in our day.

Blessings and Curses

There is little doubt that the individualism of the West has brought many blessings to us. People have been freed from the oppressive restrictions and taboos of clan and tribal life. The 'open society' permits a freedom of movement between countries and cultures. It encourages an experimentation in thought and expression which is wholesome. There is within it a highly developed sensitivity to injustice and a concern for the maximum growth and development of persons. The individualism of the West presents a barrier against totalitarian rule and provides the basis for democracy itself. It would be quite wrong to underestimate the blessings of this reality. Indeed, the genesis for much of the development of individual freedom has come from Christianity itself. The theological theme of maturity or autonomy for both individuals and institutions has given impetus to the movement towards a secular world.[3]

Nevertheless, individualism has also brought some curses. Those patterns which have developed to benefit the individual are so much taken for granted that they have given rise to a form of blindness. We cannot seem to see the greed and acquisitiveness which pervade our culture; we are blind to the aggression and stridency which accompany us upon the escalator to personal freedom; we no longer see or complain about deteriorating standards in public service; we cannot seem to see that many of our

9

important institutions such as the law, medicine, education, and the church are in decline because they lack the understanding and respect of individuals. The ugliest curse of individualism is that extreme selfishness which expresses itself not in the 'acceptance of responsibility' for others or for society, but only in the enjoyment and promotion of self. Ironically, the blindness wrought by the age of individualism makes us unable to see the very ground upon which the individual stands.

What this means is that in many countries in the West we are faced with the disintegration of community. By 'community' we simply mean those patterns of mutual concern, communication, and caring which ought to mark a shared and human life with others. The sense of belonging to a larger, coherent, and supportive whole is disappearing. The centre and hub of life is subtly shifting from a specific locale (home and neighbourhood) to an indeterminate place (workplace, car, and mobile phone or computer network). Those who are necessarily tied to the house may also be connected to a similar indeterminate network. Fewer people these days even recognise their neighbours, let alone care for them; nor do they wish to sink roots requiring effort for nurture. They wish only to be free to do their own thing, even when it merely means meandering aimlessly from one thing to another. Hence, individuals feel increasingly isolated. The age of individualism appears to be delivering not what it promised- the happy, well-adjusted, and mature person- but rather the unhappy, selfish, and lonely individual.

Pay and Display

Another recent promotion has been the idea of a 'market economy'. An emphasis on commerce and upon money as the key measure in life have accompanied this idea. The convergence of individualism and the market economy has led to a relatively new phenomenon. It can best be described as 'Consumerism' (an ugly, but suitably descriptive word). Anyone who watches television, listens to the radio, or reads newspapers and magazines will undoubtedly identify himself as a consumer. There are two important aspects to such an identity.

That aspect of consumerism tied most closely to the free market economy is that of 'ownership'. It is economically essential for people to acquire and own material things. That almost goes without saying. However, it is equally important to demonstrate to others that you do own valuable things. This is not a new insight. Long ago, the sociologist Thorsten Veblen employed the provocative term 'conspicuous consumption' to describe such behaviour. Consumption was not sufficient, Veblen argued, it also had to be seen or conspicuous. Much modern advertising is built on the foundation of conspicuous consumption. Promoting the mechanical merits of a new and upmarket car is insufficient. You really need to show off:

If you've got it, flaunt it!

Running a market economy depends on blending the desire to own things with the desire to enjoy your neighbour's envy.

Manufacturers and advertisers have learned how to accomplish this with considerable imagination and skill.

The idea of ownership, of course, is not altogether bad. To own may also imply to value and to be responsible for. Responsibility for the care and maintenance of things is therefore clearly placed upon the shoulders of the owner, who has an obvious interest in protecting what he owns. The idea is not far removed from the Christian idea of 'Stewardship'. Moreover, ownership can generate initiative and a sense of purpose, a goal in life. But it also generates competition, greed, and divisiveness. We may pour scorn on such advertising, but we usually pay attention.

The second aspect of consumerism relates to a growing emphasis on 'consumer rights'. The consumers of all goods and services are now encouraged to know and to demand their rights. Consumer programmes on the radio and television go to considerable lengths to spell out the rights of people when buying a product or receiving a service. 'Charters' have become fashionable as a way of publicising such rights.

Underlining the rights of consumers is in some respects a positive act, especially where products are concerned. People do need protection against inferior products and dubious services. The problem, however, lies in the attitude which is provoked in the consumer. People are subtly urged towards a stridency and a 'me, my, and mine' behaviour. In this way the self becomes even more strongly shifted towards the centre of life. Human relations may become highly adversarial in texture:

**My role as consumer
leaves me scant time for humour.
Pursuing my right
means I'm usually uptight.**

A more serious problem arises in relation to transactions
which have traditionally been caring in nature. Medical
practitioners, for example, are fundamentally motivated by a desire
to care for their patients. This does not mean that they are
disinterested in being rewarded for their work, but the relationship
between doctor and patient is, in the majority of cases, based on a
genuine compassion and desire to care. The injection of the
patient's 'rights' carries with it the capacity to sour the relationship.
A visit to the doctor becomes similar to a shopping expedition to
purchase a washing machine or a used car. The legalistic attitude
generated by a concern for obtaining one's rights affects both the
patient and the doctor; both may come to know their lawyer better,
and the major casualty is the quality of the relationship. The blind
drift towards consumerism promises to divide neighbours and to
adversely affect important and traditional relationships.

A Paradox of Power

Consumerism promises power to the individual, the
protection of his rights. Paradoxically, it often means
powerlessness. A 'Patient's Charter' may be on view in the surgery
waiting room or the hospital ward, but that may mean little in
practice. It provides no guarantee against the curtailment of

13

treatment due to shortage of funds, or against the closure of a hospital in spite of communal wishes, or against simple bad organisation or communication. The individual may be shown with a flourish his rights on paper, but he is often powerless to claim them in reality. This disparity between promise and delivery is a source of frustration and misery.

In other areas as well, the enunciation of consumer rights often leads not merely to frustration but to an actual deterioration in service. Ian Gilmour's post used to be delivered between 7:30 and 8:00 a.m. in the morning, early enough for him to deal with before leaving the house. Then a postal charter was produced, promising that the post would be delivered by 9:30 a.m. Indeed it is, but only just before 9:30 a.m., too late for him to receive and deal with before leaving.

Increasingly, the emphasis falls on image and presentation. So governments do not listen to the people in order to respond to real needs, but merely in order to orchestrate a better presentation of policy already cast. Talk about the rights of consumers may amount to little more than verbal gestures, leaving individuals with less control over their lives. There are two paradoxes then: when the individual is told that he has more power, he often has less; and in an age when perception is crucial, the majority accept the presentation as given, thus stumbling into the pit .

Our Unravelling Society

For many people today the very fabric of society appears to be unravelling around them. This perception does not arise from a nostalgia for a golden age which never was, but merely from exposure to the daily news and personal experience. The very seams of the society are being relentlessly unpicked by crime, violence, unemployment, poverty, widening class divisions and racial prejudice. The rehearsal of the ills of our society can be somewhat tedious. Nevertheless, it is important to try briefly to get an overview of the unravelling process. The quality press do a good job of covering the problems very thoroughly, although the cumulative effect of such coverage can be overwhelming.

Statistics about crime, as for many other social conditions, are notoriously slippery. Is crime really on the increase, or is the reportage of crime more thorough than in the past? Whatever the case, the public clearly perceive crime to be on the increase. This perception has led to a 'vigilante mentality' in certain parts of the country. A poll in Scotland indicates that 85% of Scots felt crime to be a 'serious problem' and 83% thought crime to be on the increase.[4] The prison population in Scotland has reached record levels, with more prisoners than official places for them.[5] Moreover, students of the judicial system believe that there is an increasing number of cases in the courts and that their seriousness and complexity is increasing apace.[6]

It must be clear from all this that crime is indeed perceived as a major problem in our society, and that this must have an impact upon the community. The way that people move about in society and relate to one another is affected by their estimate of personal safety and risk. In a society more 'guarded' in both a literal and figurative sense, the freedom to live and move and simply to be must surely suffer.

The social order seems also to be threatened by violence. A recent case in which two young boys aged under twelve were convicted of the abduction and murder of a toddler has for many people come to symbolise the growing reality of violence. Violence may well be associated with crime, as the statistics in respect of the criminal use of firearms would suggest; but there is also an increase in random violence, where no apparent reason may be found. It may, of course, be argued that violence has always been an intrinsic part of human life, and that we are merely witnessing it through intensive visual coverage by the media.

Violence is often associated with drug abuse, and there is now growing evidence that the use of drugs is more widespread than previously suspected. A recent inquiry by an all-party committee of Scottish MPs indicates that "... drug abuse in Scotland was a much more serious and much more extensive problem than any of us could imagine."[7]

Unemployment is also a major factor in our unravelling society. In the year 1993, 10.4% of the work force in Scotland was unemployed,[8] and yet the employment situation is Scotland is regarded as better than that in other parts of the United Kingdom. So at least one in ten people in our society has no work to do, and the picture is not expected to improve significantly for the next four years. While more and more young people are encouraged to attend college and university, the number of graduates able to find employment commensurate with their education shrinks.

Having regular employment confers that important sense of purpose, dignity, and direction required by everyone. Without work, control over one's life evaporates very quickly. Having some kind of investment or stake in the social process ensures at least a degree of participation and interest in it. Having no stake in the society induces attitudes which must further the unravelling. To put it in another way: having too much time to look for 'trouble' must ensure that some find it.

The Widening Chasm

Employment also serves as a useful tool for observing the widening divisions within society. While 'wage restraint' is promoted as a key government policy for economic recovery, such a policy appears to operate in a highly selective way. A limit of 1.5 % increase in wages has been imposed within the public sector, yet the total earnings of top company directors rose by 12 % in 1992-93.[9] The salaries of hospital trust managers rose by some 9 %, while the majority of the people they manage were subject to the same 1.5 %. In the light of this disparity the public perception must be one of an increasing division within the social order. Policies which are harsh gain credibility when applied equally, for all suffer equally; policies which are applied unequally lose their credibility very quickly.

17

There is evidence, both academic and experiential, that the traditional family unit of mother, father and children living together is also breaking down. About one-third of all marriages now end in divorce, and according to the 1991 census 17 % of all children come from single-parent families. The breakdown of the traditional family unit and the growing addiction to drugs combine to create what the MP Frank Fields has called 'social anthrax'.[10] It is a useful term, for it captures the deadly nature of the problem.

Here then is the picture of our social order as it draws near to the end of the twentieth century: a society oriented to the 'free' individual as consumer, using money as the key measure of life; a society worried by crime, obsessed by issues of law and order, and displaying high levels of unemployment, violence and drug abuse; a society marked by a widening class division between the affluent and the poor, with increasing numbers of isolated people and one-parent families; and a society in which the institutions are suffering a loss of respect. This is a fairly bleak picture, one much at odds with the preferred view of 'Great' Britain. It may be argued that we have been too pessimistic; after all, many people now enjoy a better quality of life than ever before, as we are frequently reminded. For those in a relative affluence it is quite possible to avoid the bleakness of this scene, just as it is possible to drive *around* rather than *through* the deprived sections of our cities. But our concern is for the whole of the people and the society, and so it is possible that we have been too optimistic. Our

18

impression is that a dogged adherence to our present course, with the blind leading the blind, will lead us all towards the pit.

Questions for Discussion

1. Calling upon your own experience, do you believe that society in Great Britain is becoming more or less stable? Provide some examples to illustrate.

2. What are the advantages and disadvantages of promoting individualism?

3. Exactly how has the introduction of charters changed things? Consider, for example, the National Health Service, domestic supply industries such as electricity, water and gas, and financial institutions.

4. Do you think that our picture of society at the end of the twentieth century is accurate? Why or why not?

Chapter 2

THE GAZE OF THE ONE-EYED GOD

The purpose of my remarks is to focus your attention on this little group... who [through television] wield a free hand in selecting, presenting and interpreting the great issues in our nation. They decide what forty or fifty million Americans will learn of today's events in the nation and world. We cannot measure their power and influence by traditional standards. The American people would rightly not tolerate this concentration in government. Is it not fair and relevant to question its concentration in the hands of a tiny, enclosed fraternity of privileged men, elected by no one, and enjoying a monopoly licensed and sanctioned government?--Spiro Agnew, former vice-president, the United States of America.

It is remarkable that way back in the year 1969, Spiro Agnew, not known as a particularly astute or articulate observer of society, should have seen so clearly at least one of the problems posed by the advent of television. It could be cogently argued that the major power in the world today is the electronic media: television, and to a lesser extent, radio. The media is user-friendly, which means that its power is enjoyed but not really understood, seen but not fully perceived. It exerts a profound and pervasive influence upon all institutions, governments and individuals. It colours our view of the world, affects our patterns of behaviour, and modifies our deepest beliefs and values. With considerable justification, the electronic media could be seen as the new religion of our age. Television Centre is the modern secular cathedral: it is the centre of public attention, creating and regilding images giving them power, influence and value. One striking illustration of the influence of the electronic media is the management of news, to which we now turn.

Packaging the News of the World

Any valid analysis of the electronic media must begin with the affirmation that television and radio have brought immense benefits to the world. Masses of people are informed, educated and entertained. We receive news from everywhere on the globe, including its most remote areas, and it is transmitted instantly and graphically. In many respects more people than ever before are better informed about what is happening in the world, at least in terms of the 'headline news'. A church missionary in Africa recounts the 'astonishing cultural revolution' which took place when televison arrived in the 1960's. Africans who only months before received their information from village gossip were suddenly 'aping the dress and mannerisms of U.S. television characters with total naturalness'. Informed discussions were held regarding the affairs of the world in startling fashion, and yet few knew the inhabitants of the next village.[1]

The satellite/electronic network which now encircles the world has reduced it to the proverbial global village; we know everything that goes on in the village, but whether we care is another matter. Both individuals and governments can be well-informed and thus enabled to respond to world events. The possibility of fast and appropriate responses to natural and manmade disasters is created. However, as we know with regret, the response of governments or the United Nations is not always either fast or appropriate. The new and interesting feature in this is that having viewed disaster for themselves, the populace demand a response.

The capacity of television in particular to educate is enormous. Programmes which focus on the natural world or science or on social problem have undoubtedly led to a better informed public and a heightened moral consciousness. One example is the ability of television to raise large sums of money for charity. Moreover, the capacity of television and radio to entertain is even greater. While this is a role frequently criticised, the value of high quality entertainment to lonely and isolated people can hardly be denied. The positive benefits of the electronic media are many, and it would be fair to say that we have not yet adequately understood or responsibly developed them.

However, there is also a negative side to the pervasive power of the media. It is too facile to point only to the nature of television entertainment: people are conditioned to be passive - 'couch potatoes'; soap opera and fast-moving action are favoured over subtler and more thought-provoking presentations, and communication within the home is stifled. There are many other negative factors which may not be so obvious but are more sinister. Perhaps the best example can be culled from the way that news is presented on the television.

It is clear, given some reflection, that the world news is always 'packaged' in several ways. In the first instance, there is a high degree of selectivity in presentation. Certain stories are judged to be the most important and receive greater in-depth coverage. Selectivity is hardly new; newspaper editors have always had to make decisions about the relative importance of stories. However, newspapers have more than a front page; stories judged to be of lesser import may still find a place on another page. On the whole, television presents the front page only; the lesser news has vanished. Moreover, only news with some visual interest is given substantial coverage. Assessing the weight of the news is a difficult and demanding task. It has been argued that there is a clear bias in this process towards the 'bad news'. That is, stories about conflict, violence and disaster is inevitably more provocative or appealing than 'good news'. This is hardly surprising, for it ties in with our natural inquisitiveness into all kinds of risqué areas. Colin Morris, commenting about the kind of news that intrigues and affects us, writes as follows:

The things that could do me and my little world harm are usually, though not always, more immediate, graphic and attention-grabbing than the things that might do me good. The effects of goodness are often subtle, longer-term and occur beyond the camera's range-- in the human heart, for instance.[2]

There is no question that for television the bad news is much more compelling than the good news. Morris goes on to point out that this process is enhanced by the very quality of the picture. A certain fuzziness in picture quality means that images of anger and aggression are seen more clearly than others. What all this means is that the news we see and hear provides a distorted and unbalanced view of the world. When people who are largely confined to the house and denied any direct experience of the world complain that 'the world is in an awful state', often they have merely been watching the television. This distortion of the world is bound to affect our disposition and behaviour. It would be absurd to suggest that it did not affect our perception of the world. Michael Novak comments: "The medium builds up in the viewer's mind, layer by layer, a structure of psychic expectation."[3]

The news is also packaged through the limitations imposed by time itself. Strict control over time is a natural requirement of the media. Radio and television schedules printed in the newspaper must be rigidly adhered to, at least for competitive reasons. This means that interviews or other forms of reportage are often curtailed or manipulated. A set agenda of questions may be imposed without significant reference to the responses being made. Interviewees manipulate by waffling on in order to use up the time available. The compression of news into strict time periods results finally in the 'soundbite', a mini-comment crudely extracted from its context. If the analogy is pushed, then it must be said that a few isolated bites seldom lead to a satisfying meal.

Moreover, the news is also packaged by that which precedes and follows it in the broadcasting schedule. If the news is surrounded by programmes of largely entertainment character, then to some degree it also comes to take the shape of entertainment. Thus even horrific news can make an impact roughly similar to the most mind-numbing entertainment. It is a striking thought that the sudden and unexplained disappearance of the nine o'clock news might be more upsetting to the habitual viewer than a major disaster reported by it. The packaging of the news is one of the most important aspects of media influence upon us, yet most people are largely unaware of it.

In this respect, there is a peculiar paradox in the attitude of the electronic media towards itself. On the one hand, it is recognised that television and radio have immense power, influencing attitudes and opinions, attracting money and talented personnel, and affecting the life of individuals and governments. But on the other hand, the media displays an astonishing naiveté about such power. For example, when critical questions are raised about the selection and controls of news, the answer is usually that the news department is driven purely and simply by the desire for 'truth', as if truth, like an onion, were not many-layered. Or, when criticism is expressed about the impact of television violence upon children, the answer is always that there is no evidence that such viewing harms children. The question of whether it positively benefits children is not raised. There is a significant difference between asking whether something does no harm and whether it actually does any good. This is another example of our disposition to 'whim'. In New Testament language, all things may be permissible, but not all things are helpful. The absence of an ability to be self-critical is one of the most worrying aspects of the mass media.

The Dilemma of the Absolute Present

The very nature of the way that the electronic media operate constitutes a particular problem which some have called the 'Absolute Present'. The capacity to provide instantaneous coverage of current events means that we are all being gradually conditioned to forget the past; reality is reduced to a historical vacuum. Radio and television treat us as if we had no memory of the past: that is, time is not taken to introduce the context or antecedents of events, nor is the similarity between present and past events recalled. Listeners and viewers then gain that uneasy sense of endless repetition. The continuity between present and past is lost. It is in this sense that the present becomes an absolute. The listener or viewer becomes a passive observer, unable to fit present events into the context of history or to form a meaningful view of the world. They become disabled in respect of shaping their own lives. Thus disabled, they become easy prey for whatever idea or product is being sold: "They train you to be paralysed; then they sell you crutches."4

The Absolute Present amounts to a distortion of the passage of time, but history can also be distorted in another sense. The media have it in their power both to elevate and destroy individuals, for programme material can be generated in the process. For example, the rise and fall, and rise again of Richard M. Nixon was, in part, due to the impact of the media. A very focused coverage of specific aspects of a person's life gives rise to such power. In this sense the media sometimes operate as king-makers or destroyers.

Questions may also be raised about the role of the media in the political process itself. Much coverage is focused upon politics in terms of news. This is a phenomenon especially pronounced in Great Britain. The television and radio reportage of politics is continuous and intense, and this attention clearly changes the nature of the political process. The news media are in turn manipulative and manipulated. Documents are 'leaked' in order to judge public reaction to proposed policies or to embarrass another party. All parties now display an increased ability to use the media for their own ends. On the other hand, as we have already seen, the media also manipulate the parties. In the United States, the continuous and relentless probing of the 'Whitewater Affair' eventually forced President Clinton to establish a special investigator to look into the matter. It may be argued, of course, that in this sense the media act as a guardian of democracy by providing a check upon the politicians. However the role of the media in the political sphere is regarded, the fact that it is a powerful force transforming the democratic process is now undeniable.

The Power of Image

If the news often distorts our view of the world, then those images presented through television and the cinema have in a more general sense an even greater power to distort life. One of the insights gained by the Beirut hostages was of the power that the images held over their captors. Brian Keenan recalls visiting a cinema in Beirut to watch a rather meaningless war film set in Vietnam. He writes about the experience as follows:

We sat there in the darkened cinema and as each character pulled out his weapon and began firing furiously, the young Arab men around us groan and moan in a kind of ecstasy, crying out the names of the weapons. All round us in the cinema we would hear the words, 'Kalashnikov, Kalashnikov; Beretta, Beretta!' These young men knew the names of every type of gun, even the names of mortars and rocket launchers. The cinema rang with a chant of excited worship.[5]

Keenan goes on to say much more about the power of the visual image. The hostages' captors believed that the images they saw on the cinema or television screen were accurate portrayals of Western life. The cultural variety of the West had for them been summed up under a single visual image. The captors had difficulty reconciling the reality of the persons they held hostage with their received images of Westerners. As the visual 'image' becomes pervasive through the world, its ultimate impact on differing cultures may be uncertain, but its power to influence is not. It reduces the uniqueness of the individual and homogenises the cultural variety of the world.

Finally, the rapidly expanding network of communication systems raise new possibilities and problems. As satellite and cable adds to the number of channels available it may well offer alternative versions of reality and act as a spur to the growth of the human spirit. On the other hand, it may equally permit the concentration of immense power in the hands of a few people. In a number of parts of the world the media is owned and controlled by multinational companies, and in a market economy such power is ripe for manipulation. Is this not the vision of Spiro Agnew, but played now on the wide screen? Who will control our view of the world, and to what end? Who can withstand the gaze of the one-eyed god?

Questions for Discussion

1. What parallels can you find between television and religion?

2. Does television affect the democratic process? Watch the evening news bulletin and take note of its content. Compare it the next day with the coverage in a quality newspaper, asking why items are included or excluded.

3. Is the presentation of news a vital ingredient in the protection of democracy? If so, how?

4. Will the power of the visual image increase or decrease during the next decade, and what will the consequences be?

Chapter 3

FATAL ATTRACTIONS

"Sun, Sea, Sex, and Violence"-- Title on the spine of *GQ Male Magazine- Gentlemen's Quarterly*.

It is obvious that mass communication, in and of itself, is neither good nor bad. It is simply one force, albeit a powerful one, at work in society. It can be used to stimulate good, healthy, responsible relationships and attitudes, or the reverse. While in British society we continue to buy a large quantity of newspapers (though now gradually declining), more and more magazines are being published and purchased. The variety and quantity of magazines on the shelves of a good newsagent is now somewhat bewildering. Like the electronic media, newspapers and magazines have a profound influence upon the thoughts, feelings and actions of their readers. Because of this influence, questions must be raised about the power exercised by this section of the media, and its impact on both individuals and on society.

In this century the most astute manipulator of the media was Adolf Hitler. He was aware that the vast majority of human

31

behaviour is not determined by rational thought or experience but by feelings and unconscious drives. Albert Speer, his Minister of Armaments, described his methods after the end of the War: "It was a dictatorship which made use of all technical means for the domination... eighty million people were deprived of independent thought... subject to the will of one man." Our current society is hardly on the same basis as that in Germany in the 1930's. Even so, the potential power available through the sale of newspapers and magazines means that one ideological group could gain great influence with voters, as well as establishing patterns of behaviour and reinforcing standards either good or bad. To what extent are we being deprived of independent thought?

Selling Sex

There are several different ways of selling newspapers and magazines. Clearly the most popular way is to make use of erotica or sex. The fact is that sex sells. It sells products of all kinds and also the publications in which such products are advertised. Both men and women are targeted. If our instincts can be inflamed then our sales resistance can be lowered. The formula may be obvious but it is also extremely powerful: it is to engender an increased craving for a product which actually delivers little long-term satisfaction. Some publications in which sex has been implicit in the past now focus quite explicitly on the subject. This is particularly true of magazines for women such as *Cosmopolitan.* The rationale for such a focus is that sexual relationships are natural and normal and so ought to be discussed freely at home, at

32

work, and, of course, in magazines. A further specialisation is the sexual problems page, with answers provided by an 'agony aunt'. The provision for advice on sexual problems is fast becoming a growth industry. Is this because we truly believe that such advice will solve our problems, or only because we secretly relish and enjoy the misfortunes of others?

The 'S' word also becomes the search word for newspaper stories. Stories are sought about the sexual exploits of 'Casanovas', television soap stars, and ministers (cabinet and religious). Such stories often have a profound effect: top headlines are garnered for a while, libel cases are raised in court, and important people may be brought down., whether or not their 'indiscretions' bear any relation to their role. A great opportunity is provided for those who decide to 'kiss and tell'. For what was 'sex scandal' in the past we may now often read 'fiscal opportunity'.

When sex is given so much space and significance it often produces an unhealthy environment. All relationships come to be judged on the content and/or quality of the 'intimate' factor. This creates pressure to gain sexual experience at an earlier age or at an earlier stage in a relationship, producing stresses and strains in turn. Moreover, the reader is given the impression that everyone (except him or her) enjoys a marvellous sex life with a multitude of gorgeous partners.

The rich and famous also are easy targets for exploitation. Britain's royal family are continuously targeted by several magazines, as well as newspapers. The extent to which such publications will go illustrates the hyped-up attraction which the coming and going of the famous and rich have for many in our culture. Hidden cameras with telephoto lens invade privacy in order to 'create' a story. This invasion of private space is a constant source of anxiety and misery for many. The sound of picture-taking and story-telling is the sound of money changing hands.

The church is also a soft target for the media. By nature a fairly conservative body with a wide spectrum of personalities and opinions within its ranks, the church may always be found to be out of step with the times or found to harbour some minister making extreme statements about any topic under the sun. It is a simple matter to stereotype the 'Non-believing Bishop' or the 'Vicar who ran off with the Organist' or the 'Embezzler Treasurer'. The church can be taken off the peg any day, any month, when other news is rare. The declining membership, or conflicts over doctrines, or rows between the minister and Kirk Session can be employed to illustrate the 'inevitable' decline of the church. To be fair, the newspapers do reliably print material provided by the church in terms of press releases. But not a great deal of effort is made to discover and report more interesting and important news about the life and activity of the church. The amount of coverage given to the church in any positive sense does not compare with the coverage given to minority sports or even to fashion..

One example may help to illustrate the media approach to the church. In the 1960's, a poorly organised collection for Christian Aid in the Easterhouse area near Glasgow raised only 50 pounds.

This event received derisory publicity in the *Daily Record*. A short time later a second collection was made, but this time it was well organised and the total sum raised was in excess of 700 pounds, fourteen times as much. However, this event was not regarded as newsworthy and so received no coverage.

The Fun House

The tabloid press in particular and some magazines offer a voyage into the fun house in an amusement arcade. The fun house contains a variety of mirrors which distort our own images, producing a fat or a thin person or a tall or a short one. The airjet blows the girls dresses up over their heads, producing embarrassment and gales of laughter. During the ride through the darkened house of mystery, skeletons and grotesque images leap out of the dark to frighten or alarm. The fun house offers a distorted world which entertains, amuses, and frightens, but it is a closed and superficial world. You exit exactly where you entered. For some, this kind of coverage may entertain, amuse and alarm, but it seldom moves them forward in understanding. A distorted world is presented, a world where fame, sex, and wealth are portrayed as the main values in society. If such publications were presented as comics they might be tolerated, but they are disguised as 'news'. Moreover, by such a presentation, everyone appears to be extreme in behaviour and attitude. Thus ignorance about more normal aspects of life is actually encouraged. By tapping the dark side of human nature, the media cynically encourage the baser instincts such as lust for sex, power and money. While exploiting "sun, sea, sex and violence", they never hint that such things could amount to fatal attractions for many. This view is shared by many responsible journalists as well. For example, writing about how the 'sad tabloid pages' can help us read the 'nation's mind', Joyce McMillan comments:

> It's clear... that the tabloids trade on the sexual repressions of a society which, for all the public chat about 'permissiveness', continues to find the whole subject immensely shocking and titillating. They trade on a profound streak of violence and rage in our culture, which seems to have its roots in the family--sexual repression and prurience, suppress violence and rage, fear, anxiety, a profound sense of loss...[1]

Such an analysis leads inevitably to the thorny question of censorship. Conducting informed debate about censorship is notoriously difficult. On the one hand, it would appear to be a relatively easy matter to ban gratuitous stories which appear to have no redeeming value. It is, however, difficult to draw a line between materials having or not having socially redeeming value. Censorship is always authoritarian and thus threatens the 'open' society. Moreover, we already have wide experience of the impact of banning things. Prohibition may lead simply to an under-the-counter market which benefits cunning entrepreneurs.

The goal posts have shifted, with greater pressure being applied to editors to sell copies. Consider the formally douse magazine *Woman's Own*. In the August 1994 issue its cover stories included: "The day Mum told me she was gay", "How could you kill our children?", and "Tranquillisers turned me from this...to THIS" Freedom and responsibility are dependent upon each other; freedom and avarice are not. Too often the rightly valued 'Freedom of the Press' has been used as a rubric to cover many sins. Too many people have been cruelly treated for the sake of a headline. As one affected person wrote about our free press in this country: "...free to cause embarrassment, confusion and pain to helpless and unsuspecting people."[2]

All sections of the media today exercise great power over both society and individuals. They have the power either to distort or to clarify the social order and the political process. An irresponsible intrusion into some social processes may well have serious repercussions. Detective Superintendent John Bennett,who was in charge of the investigations relating to the Cromwell Road murders in Gloucester, indicated his practical difficulties: "Some media activities are frustrating my inquiry. There appeared to be no depths some will go to in order to create sensationalism with speculation, misrepresentation and exaggeration, which I believe is unethical and morally wrong."[3]

There are several fatal attractions in operation. To use shock tactics, the horror angle, or an over-emphasis on the titillating, to outsell rivals in the market place may make business sense. Sadly, it takes no account of the climate such 'reporting' creates. There are many easily influenced people, young and old, who believe such attitudes and incidents are typical of the rest of society.

37

The use and abuse of power is more worrying. The very survival of society depends upon the ability of large numbers of people making rational and realistic choices in the light of accurate information. We are dependent, like it or lump it, on adequate and accurate information appearing in the 'black and white of newsprint'. If a publication has a political bias and a high circulation, it may prove tempting to move into the area of propaganda, telling us to accept as self-evident matters about which it would be more prudent to suspend judgement.

In certain parts of this world the media is merely the voice piece of the state. Fortunately, in Britain, we retain more freedom, though the news media potentially can be manipulated by those able to purchase a controlling interest. Certain philosophies can then be pushed, be they political or social.

Newspapers and magazines have massive influence at this time which not even they appear to appreciate, nor always use sensitively or responsibly. When games are played in the Fun House it is the weakest, those having the least willpower and critical assessment, who are most at risk. However, as the climate subtly changes under such influence, all of us will see and feel the differences in our streets, shopping centres, and personal relationships.

Questions for Discussion

1. Hitler was one astute manipulator of the media. Can you think

of individuals and groups today who wish to manipulate the media?

2. Why do individuals, companies and governments wish to control the media? Be as specific as possible.

3. To what extent does the media's distortion of the world affect the thinking and behaviour of people and especially younger people? Give some examples.

4. Discuss and elaborate on the gains and losses for society through a more open presentation of sexual issues.

5. According to Alistair Cooke, the task of the journalist is to "Comfort the afflicted and afflict the comfortable." Do you believe that the majority of journalists match that criterion?

PART II

PERSPECTIVES ON THE CHURCH

Chapter 4

WOMB WITHOUT A VIEW

The people will listen and listen, but not understand; they will look and look, but not see.-- Isaiah the prophet.

While the world is heading towards the pit through a lack of vision, the church does have access to a vision of life capable of rescuing it. The problem is that the church neither adheres to its own vision nor projects it for the sake of the world. One of the key reasons for this failure is that it is preoccupied with itself. Being in the church is remarkably like being in the womb. It is safe and protective. The walls around are familiar and comforting. A regular supply of well-worn ideas, oft-repeated phrases, and recognised patterns keep members relatively happy. While some may occasionally show signs of impatience and rebellion and kick out at the walls, such blows are limited in force and intent. The church, like the womb, is thought of as a sphere in which we live in security. It is not regarded as a realm which one would wish either to change or to leave. As the foetus inside the womb can only view it from inside, so many in the church only see it from inside. They carry little sense of its real purpose, and even less desire to reshape it. For many church people, including many

41

leaders, the goal finally becomes to loiter in the church without intent. Ralph Morton and Mark Gibbs comment: "The church is in serious danger of becoming the psychological refuge of elderly people who are unhappy about the pace of change in the modern world... oriented to the Victorian past and not to the future at all."[1]

There is, of course, not much wrong with the desire to find security, community, and personal fulfilment in the church, for it is in its deepest and best sense all about community. Indeed, the individualism about which we spoke in the first chapter cries out for correction by the church. Yet the womb-like atmosphere stifles any sense that the church is an institution in need of sharpening for the sake of the world. Thus precious little reform is undertaken. The Reformers of the sixteenth century called for the church always to be reforming itself in the light of the scriptures. This Reformation principle is often affirmed in ringing terms but seldom applied in practice. When the Moderator of the General Assembly is led into the assembly hall on the Mound, to be followed by the glorious singing of the 'Old Hundredth' all thoughts of rational reform dissolve in the grandeur of tradition. The structures and patterns established of old hold such sway that significant change is next to impossible. It is much easier to accept life in the womb than to undergo birthing into a harsh world. This often the case even for those who do not wish to loiter in the womb.

A Presbyterian who has spent many years studying and writing about church and ministry in another country spent some time observing the church in Scotland and talking to its ministers. He noted in particular the absence of any impetus to change. When asked for his opinion of the ministers as key agents of reform , he said simply: "They have given up, haven't they?". The 'giving up' to his mind did not imply a loss of faith or lack of commitment by ministers; rather it reflected a high degree of hopelessness about changing the church into the kind of community it ought to be. The failure of the church to respond positively to creative initiatives produces inertia in its leaders.

One of the important New Testament metaphors for the church is that of an 'earthen vessel'. The implication is that it ought to be capable of being shaped like a piece of pottery to serve the purpose of God.[2] But this is hardly the view that many church people and leaders hold. The practices and procedures of the institution are granted a sacred attribute which makes them highly resistant to change. Thus the sacraments become "*Holy* Baptism" and "*Holy* Communion". The ministry becomes the "*Holy* Ministry", and ministers come to think of themselves as set apart in status and not simply in function. This inability to view the church as an institution requiring, like all other human institutions, to be altered to increase its effectiveness means that it grows more remote and ineffective in a rapidly changing world.

A Marginal Church

Near the end of the twentieth century, what we see is a church pushed to the very margins of life. To say this is not in any sense to suggest that the church ought to be conforming to the

43

fashions of this world. The message of the crucifixion and resurrection of Jesus is and ought to be a scandal which is unacceptable to many. But the context and form in which that message is presented has too often simply an old-fashioned aroma. That is, in an age when people are attuned to movement and colour and mutual communication, the church all too often is sunk in inertia, dressed in black and heard speaking in a monologue. When the rest of the world is sprinting in trainers the church is plodding along in heavy black boots. The prediction of Martin Luther King was chilling in its accuracy: "If the church of today does not recapture the sacrificial spirit of the early church it will lose the authentic ring and be dismissed as an irrelevant social club with no meaning."[3]

Being in the church, like being in the womb, often means being detached from the real world, at least in a mental sense. Some ministers and members alike often think in terms of practices and styles of life which held in the past but no longer hold today. One example is that of ministerial visitation to people in their homes. For many this is still regarded as a very important aspect of ministry, and the failure to visit is often given as an explanation in part for the church's decline. Yet the reality is that the nature of life, work and the home today means that often there are many fewer people at home to visit. The subtle shift from a determinate place in the home and local community to an indeterminate centre of life has undercut an older pattern of ministry. Spending time training others to visit would be a much better use of the minister's time. In many congregations 'worship' means champing rather unconsciously through a received diet of hymn prayer lesson sermon offering without much regard for the intelligence or digestion of the people. There are many such patterns or mind-sets, not related directly to the gospel, which once were appropriate but are no longer so. The failure to apply a 'real world' mentality helps to ensure that the church remains on the margins of life.

On the whole, the media present a negative view of the church. The pattern of reporting on a barrage of press releases and committee reports at predictable times in the church year induces both boredom and gloom. Undoubtedly this is due in part to a failure of the church's own public relations effort. Meanwhile, the more interesting good news of the work of congregations and other groups is often not conveyed to the press. Both locally and nationally, the church has not presented itself in appropriate and positive ways to journalists. At the same time, at least in Scotland, there is a very peculiar compound of secular patriotism and paternalistic cynicism directed at the 'Kirk'. Little in-depth journalism is done to discover what is actually happening in many lively and vital congregations, and the kind of journalistic expertise which is expended or business or the arts or the society is rarely exercised on the subject of religion. Moreover, the media enjoys nothing more than discovering 'rows' and scandals. While these are looked for in all areas of life, they give rise to a special form of glee in this more 'sacred' setting.

45

The failure of the media to provide a complete and thus fair picture of the church means that a growing secularity is strengthened. Those who are already detached from the life of the church are not informed in a way that might modify their detachment. There is no longer any common language for the mutual discussion of theology. The detachment of so many means that worship in the church is often a peculiar affair, no matter how well it is planned and executed. At services which include the sacrament of baptism, numerous relatives and friends of the family arrive who know next to nothing about hymns, lessons, creeds, or basic etiquette. At church weddings guests arrive whose main intent is to record the service via video or flash photograph. rather than enjoy it.

"Oh what a beautiful baby!"- A visitor.
"That's nothing. You should see his photograph!"
- His mother.

This growing secularity and ignorance about the church has several implications. In the first place it means that no matter how well things are done in the church or how lively and vital it is, there is no effective way of communicating this to the outside world. Thus many people are surprised that a congregation is alive, vital and healthy, and that their friends actually attend! These days anyone who wishes to join the church by attending a membership class must first overcome the hurdles of disbelief and disapproval by their friends. In the second place it means that ministers increasingly are forced into an 'official' role at various social rites or rituals. For example, the minister is asked to conduct funerals even when no one, not even the deceased, would wish for any Christian content. What is wanted is not meaningful content in the important events of life but merely official 'gestures'.

The harsh secularity of the world, plus the increasing detachment of people from the church, plus the womb-like mentality of the church itself make up a deadly cocktail, whether shaken or stirred. These factors lessen the ability of the church to carry out an adequate prophetic role in the life of the world. There has been some excellent work undertaken by the Church and Nation Committee of the Church of Scotland and by other leading activists, academics and church leaders. While such genuine and helpful contributions cannot be ignored, they are often devalued because they are probably far removed from the thinking of many members.

Only when the whole church awakens from its slumbers, escapes from its preoccupation with self, and emerges from the comfort of the womb will its constructive proclamation be taken seriously. It is precisely then that a church on the margin could use that new position creatively to speak with and on behalf of those group and individuals who have also been pushed to the outer edges of our society.

Questions for Discussion

1. Do you find it helpful to compare the church to the womb?

Where does the analogy hold true and where does it fail?

2. Often change within the church has not been effected by the decisions of one leader, committee, or Assembly, but rather through the witness of pioneering individuals or small groups who have quietly attempted new things. What is the priority for new developments today? Who should initiate them?

3. Which is more accurate: to say that the church is being pushed to the margins of society or to say that it is simply being ignored by society?

4. How should the church communicate its message to an increasingly secular society?

Chapter 5

CLOCK WITHOUT HANDS

"Her wheels move endlessly, but we have forgotten what they are supposed to indicate or what purpose they are supposed to serve"-- D. Allan Easton

The church has a vision of the world which has the power and clarity to transform it for the better. That the church's role is to transform the world was a central affirmation of John Calvin. In Geneva during the Reformation Calvin sought rigorously to bring every aspect of life under the rule of God. He developed plans and structures to transform government, education and community life in general. Obviously, not everyone was happy under this rather strict regime. Nevertheless, he at least had a clear vision of what the world should be and the firm resolve to implement it. Yet today, for many at least, being in the church is indeed like being in a womb; there is no clear view of the world as it is or as it should be, and little resolve to change anything.

In this chapter we take a more intensive look at the reasons for this phenomenon. Way back in the years 1945-46, Allan

Easton, who was minister of the Old Kirk in Edinburgh could write the following:

> Deprived of her vision the Church of Scotland has become a piece of very complicated machinery, ceaselessly turning for the sake of turning. Her wheels move endlessly, but we have forgotten what they are supposed to indicate or what purpose they are meant to serve. We keep doing the things which we have always done and which we believe our fathers have done before us. Asked for our reasons for doing so, we all too often have none to offer.[1]

It would be nearly impossible to exaggerate the prophetic nature of Easton's words. Fifty years later precisely the same comment could be made about the church, for little has changed! If the piece of machinery referred to by Easton is thought of as a clock, then the church may be thought of as an antique and well-maintained clock, but without hands-- ticking over nicely but pointing to nothing.

The use of the clock as an analogy for the church is very appropriate, and it is worthwhile pursuing it further. What we say in this chapter provides, we hope, a fairly accurate picture of the Church of Scotland in particular, but of the whole church as well. As an ancient, venerable, and rather sophisticated piece of machinery the church offers much to admire and respect. Those structures which are in place to keep the mechanism ticking over are elaborate and impressive. The Church of Scotland has an elaborate structure for governing the whole church: the local

50

congregation is governed by the Kirk Session, the Kirk Session by the Presbytery, and the Presbytery by the General Assembly. A way into this structure may be found in the *Blue Book*, which is the official collection of committee reports to the General Assembly of the church. In the year 1993 the *Blue Book* contained over seven hundred pages . The amount of time and effort required to produce such a volume each and every year is enormous. Those committees of the Assembly which study issues and produce such reports are democratically organised and contain both lay and ministerial members.

The trouble is that if such committees and their secretariat are considered as the 'wheels' of the church, then it must be said that the wheels turn ominously slowly, and their cogs seldom merge with those of other committees. That is to say that one committee responsible for various aspects of the church life is often not aware of what another committee is doing. Very little takes place in the way of rational integration of differing areas of the church's ministry. So, for example, the large brown envelope that lands upon ministers' desks each month contains a number of unrelated missives from separate departments. Where one might long for one document to publicise and update us about the work of the church, there are many, which is highly disconcerting. There is an uneasy feeling that much labour and time is spent on deliberation, decision-making and report producing without much real advance. The means have subtly and systematically replaced the ends. This is simply to say that the church is, not surprisingly, like other bureaucratic institutions. While the committee structure involves many people, is democratic and ensures that decisions are not hastily made, it moves too slowly in a very rapidly changing world. At the end of the day it tends to frustrate and alienate those very people who have most to offer. The wheels keep turning, but the device points to nothing in or for the world.

Ideal versus Real

One reason for this is the failure to take the church seriously as a human institution. On the one hand, under the influence of a particular theology, it has been seen as a 'Royal Priesthood'. That is, the church has been regarded as an ideal above and beyond the church building on the corner. The theory has been that if the theology is right the church should flourish. At the same time, the church structure has been simply accepted as a historical/legal institution which must adhere to long-established procedures. Very little has been done to integrate the ideal image with the existing structures. Thus there is no comprehensive view of the church as a human body having a divine purpose. Had there been a framework which provided an impetus to study the church as an institution similar to other institutions, some of the mechanics could have been repaired or updated.

It has long been a cardinal principle in the Presbyterian church that things should be done 'decently and in order'. There is little doubt that this has been achieved. The clock is orderly, even if it points nowhere. The problem is that at many different levels the order imposes a forbidding regime on both ministers and members. The 'courts' of the church are exceedingly well named, for they do in fact operate much like law courts, where one might be held in contempt for speaking out of order. For many people the awesome nature of meetings ensures that they will not feel able to contribute. This often means that those who have through time overcome their inhibitions will effectively dominate proceedings. For the most part this means ministers.

Even at the level of the congregation, order can be a persistent problem. Presbyterian services are worship are usually beautifully ordered. Thus certain patterns of worship become so ingrained that they drain a service of all freedom and vitality. A mind-set is formed: if this order is followed and completed, then we will have worshipped. All questions about the meaning and relevancy of worship are in this way stifled. If we have passed an hour in this setting, then we must surely have worshipped! An order of worship in this sense takes on the quality of the sacred by habitual repetition and so can not be questioned or altered.

The Tyranny of Words

Continuing at the level of worship in the church, the verbal is apt to tyrannise just as effectively as order. The Presbyterian church is also respected for its insistence upon an educated ministry. There is much to be grateful for in this sense, and history is marked with good examples of the benefits of such a ministry. Nevertheless, there can be and usually is a tyranny of words which marks worship. Almost all the elements of worship are verbal in nature: hymns, prayers, lessons, and sermon. There is little that is intentionally non-verbal or dramatic. The worshipper in the pew would normally expect to 'see' a very static picture: a man or a woman in black stationary in a pulpit or at a table or lectern. This is not a very stimulating visual image when most of us are accustomed to 'moving pictures' in colour on the cinema and television screen.

The Presbyterian church also boasts another excellent tradition: the 'Priesthood of all Believers'. It was a Reformation principle that all Christians had a priesthood or ministry. Some might be called to exercise a specialised ministry of 'Word and Sacrament', but this role was to differ only in function and not in status . This is another dictum that we affirm in principle but rarely keep in practice. Ministers dominate worship, dominate Presbytery meetings and dominate the General Assembly. They convene committees and moderate meetings of the court. The 'Priesthood of Some Believers' is now tacitly accepted by all. Elders and Deacons/nesses offer little complaint when they are segregated at services of ordination and not permitted to lay on hands to ordain.

The Resurrection is Central

There are theological problems of self-understanding as well. We shall attempt only to focus on one, but one which is central to the church. One of the acts of worship which the Church of Scotland continues to do 'well' is the sacrament of communion. In most churches, communion is celebrated four times a year, and in some churches less. But it tends to be a grand occasion. Elders visit their districts and take out communion cards, which are invitations to attend, but also handy for keeping records. Attendance at communion is often high, the atmosphere rather formal with a sense that something important is happening.

Yet it is also true that for the most part the worship at services of communion focuses upon the death of Christ rather than his resurrection. While the service normally contains words and phrases pertaining to the resurrection, and while the resurrection may be in the mind of the minister and others, the focus is really on death for most. To illustrate this, it is our experience that when communion falls on Easter Sunday, worship is perceived by many as 'problem'. "How can we celebrate Easter when communion is about the death of Christ?" is the way the question is framed. As a further illustration, it is instructive to note the Easter hymns in the hymnbook. Most are about 'Easter Day' rather than about the resurrection as a persistent and central theme in faith and worship. This stands in sharp contrast to the crucifixion hymns, which are not so seasonally limited.

The point is that the central and main focus of the faith of the church of Scotland appears to be the cross and the death of Christ rather than the resurrection. This contradicts the faith of the early church, for whom the resurrection is central and all important. But the 'successful' nature of the service of communion in the life of the church means that it is a reinforced pattern in its worship life. The act of worship which we do best of all is the very thing which drives home a flawed theology. This is a subtle point, and one which is not easily identified precisely because it a pattern so firmly entrenched. Yet it would be difficult to overstate its importance. To focus upon the death of Christ produces quite a different outlook and expectation than a focus upon the risen Christ. Much in the Church of Scotland might be illuminated by this theological error.

It would be very wrong to suggest that there is no new life to be seen in the church. Indeed, there is much that is positive, vital and exciting. However, most of these things happen in the life of congregations across the land. For this reason, the general picture of a church in perpetual decline is highly inaccurate. Many congregations enjoy a lively and relevant worship, and are essential to the life of their surrounding community. But their vitality exists not because of the larger institution but rather in spite of it. The mechanism of the whole church helps to regularise their existence in some ways, but it does little to support or encourage them, and it certainly does not learn from them. It enlists the talent and money from such congregations for the purpose of keeping the clock ticking, but it does little to stimulate and encourage the growth and development of the congregation.

Perhaps it is not surprising that the church as an institution is in need of an overhaul. It has, after all, been running for well over four hundred years since the Reformation. It is more surprising that it is still ticking at all. Many other institutions of the sixteenth century have long ago passed into oblivion. It would be good to refit the hands so that they pointed boldly to what the world should be under the rule of God. It would be good if the mechanism of the church made possible the nurturing and the sharing of the signs of new life which do exist across Scotland. It would be good if the clock were so carefully, lovingly, and courageously overhauled that it clearly signified the divine purpose.

Questions for Discussion

1. From the perspective of the New Testament, what is the purpose of the church? Is it fulfilling it? Why or why not?

2. Specify the advantages and disadvantages of government by committees and larger bodies such as the Presbytery and the General Assembly.

3. Do you think that ordained ministers exert too much influence in the church? What kinds of pressures do they bring to bear?

4. Do you agree with the proposition that the church is centred too much upon the death of Christ rather the resurrection? Study the section entitled "Christ's Resurrection and Exaltation" in the hymnbook. How many hymns could be used throughout the year rather than only on "Easter Day"?

Chapter 6

A NARROWING PANORAMA
OR
"HEY DAD, WE SHRANK THE CHURCH"

**The time has come for judgement to begin with the
household of God-- 1 Peter 4:7**

Tense Future (A Little Vignette)

Having enjoyed a 'Decade of Evangelism' in the 1990's,
during which the membership of the church declined faster than
ever before, we moved into the first decade of the 21st century to
the 'Decade of Ministry'. It was so titled by the General Assembly
of 1999 in an attempt to attract a different breed of minister by
offering higher stipends. It proved very successful, for the new
candidates who flocked to be selected had one thing in common: a
desire for bigger and bigger stipends. By the year 2005 the
ordinary members had re-titled it 'The decade of Mammon'. The
idea was discussed again at the Assembly of 2008, when it was
appreciated that stipends were twice the national average of a
white collar worker's salary. The specific proposal which led to the
end of the Ministry/Mammon period was that one to issue every

minister a top of the range Mercedes. Having rejected this commitment to avarice (by a narrow majority), the church stumbled into a decade of self-questioning under the official rubric of 'Ten Years to Consider Where On Earth the Church is Heading'. During that significant time, *ad hoc* committees multiplied rapidly, many intelligent reports were written, and many good and heated debates were held. Agreement was finally reached on certain basics: day-glo dog collars for ministers, a new church logo- 'A Living Flame'- sponsored by British Gas, and a request that every member leave one-tenth of his estate after death to the Kirk. One tabloid newspaper was sued for a dubious report that one Kirk Session had prayed for its richer members to die sooner rather than later. A more determined and theologically sound position was taken upon entering the 2020's, which was named the 'Decade of Confession'. The main content of suggested publicity, prayers and sermons could be crudely summarised as "Hey Dad, we shrank the church. Sorry!"

Tense Present (The Way Things Are)

It is important to make a rational attempt to predict the church's course over the next years. The membership of the church is decreasing at a growing rate. In the year 1993 the total decrease amounted to nearly 20,000. In the ten year period from 1984 the total decrease has been 171,156.[1] As membership declines, the available resources dwindle. While overall contributions to the church have increased, and the offering per member has increased, the giving "...is still not allowing maintenance of existing work and certainly not providing additional income for new work."[2] The money shortfall between allocations and receipts is increasing, and amounted to 4.19 % in 1992.[3] There is no discernible reason to expect any reversal of this trend. Statistics are not everything, of course. It could be argued that the process of shrinkage is healthy in that the 'dead wood' is falling, leaving a smaller but more vital membership. Indeed, it could also be argued that the preaching of the gospel is a scandal which most people cannot accept. But there is no evidence to support the view that the church is becoming more relevant and vital in the world or that its preaching has been sharpened to express the cutting edge of the gospel. To the contrary, the report of the Panel on Worship finds it necessary to comment as follows: "Boredom in worship is a lethal sin, especially when it reduces the congregation to being apathetic spectators rather than active participants."[4]

As the church's resources dwindle, the shrinking process will hasten. This slow contraction will affect the more vulnerable aspects of its life first. Congregations which are unable to be financially viable, such as in rural areas and in housing schemes, may be united or dissolved, with a devastating effect on their surrounding communities. Finance is often a poor criterion for judging the success of a congregation's witness. Some of the more imaginative and experimental projects are also likely to go, like community ministry, overseas aid, and chaplaincy work. The bureaucracy of the church may be marginally affected but, like all bureaucracies, will be less vulnerable to the pruning hook. Those congregations which are stronger financially will continue to shrink but endure for some considerable time. The loyalty of people to their 'Kirk' is impressive, even as outsiders jeer "Hey folks, you shrank the church."

As church members are asked to contribute more generously of their resources there will indeed be a degree of renewal. Sacrifice often does produces increased commitment. New projects will be introduced, and some congregations will buck the trend by bringing a degree of creativity to the tasks, taking risks and attracting members. There are, however, limits to this process. The allocation of resources will be more narrowly focused upon the preservation of the individual congregation. Giving for the wider work of the church will not prove so popular. As we write there are proposals before the General Assembly of 1994 to insist that congregations which are vacant but in debt may not be given permission to call a minister. Stipends are to be increased substantially over the next few years.

Overall, these policies imply an increased preoccupation with money and plant and hence with self-preservation. They also imply the centralisation of churches. There will be fewer churches serving larger areas and employing a larger and more professional staff. This may succeed in providing livelier and better organised congregations for some members (those prepared and able to travel a greater distance), but it will leave more people remote and detached from the living focus of the church. It will certainly signal a major shift from the historical image of the Kirk as the shepherd of all the people. Indeed, it might be a good time to detach the label 'National Church' from the Church of Scotland, for the 'local congregation' would be a historical relic.

These changes would be very destructive for whole communities of church and non-church people alike who live in rural or urban priority areas. The Church of Scotland has been respected, with justification, for establishing congregations in nearly every new area of the country. For the church to withdraw from such areas would constitute a failure of faith and commitment to the people of Scotland. It is a vital, though not always valued, contribution to the life of every community when an identifiable group of people meet on a regular basis in worship to celebrate God's gifts and express their concerns and plans for their area.

The dwindling influence of the more traditional and broadly based congregations in Scotland (holding together a wide range of theological and political viewpoints) means that the fundamentalist wing of the church could gain more influence. There does appear to be more candidates with such views entering the ministry than in the past. Their narrower and literal interpretation of scripture, coupled with a simplistic, black and white approach to morality is likely to attract only those with similar views. Thus the fundamentalist approach in many congregations, added to a mass ignorance of the faith in the larger community will reduce the chances of finding a reasoned and critical personal faith. Moreover, the common fundamentalist tendency to axe all 'merely social' activities which are not strictly 'religious' will provide another body blow to community. Paradoxically, this may well open the door much wider for other religions and pseudo-religions. The absence of a lively, yet critically considered expression of the faith will cause some who are genuinely seeking a deeper insight into life to look to other faiths.

It is possible, then, to project a society largely devoid of the voice of the historic church. A shrunken and introverted institution will sound increasingly shrill and be seen to be marching more and more out of step. As society and the world become increasingly dominated by the media and multinational companies, there will be few voices to challenge prevailing fashions and offer alternative values and views. While it may be argued that the media does at least express a variety of viewpoints, it also displays a united resolve to maintain its power. Without a church strong enough or perceptive enough to express an alternative view of reality, we face the prospect of an secular, homogenised world.

Tense Past (A Historical Vignette)

The Reformers of the sixteenth century faced seemingly intractable and endemic problems, such as clericalism, ecclesiastical corruption, and a lust for power and money by short-sighted leaders, but they discovered the will to make those radical alterations required to permit the church to serve God in a disciplined way. Speaking of such times, the theologian Robert McAfee Brown, puts it this way: "This is the secret of the Reformation. In faithfulness to Christ the church said 'no' to much of its own life- and was thereby redeemed. The tragedy would be for people to say today: "The reformation has been finished."[5]

It is remarkable that the shrinking of the church produces such ecclesiastical paralysis. An uncritical reliance on certain traditions plus an inability to treat the church as a human institution capable of creative change means that we are unable to deal with the current crisis. From a Reformed perspective, such a paralysis seems inappropriate Have our oft-affirmed principles of dependence upon scripture and a readiness to reform the church been sacrificed forever?.

One of the ancient proverbs of the Jewish faith is "if your goals are good you will be respected." The church in Scotland has been supported by the people of this country when its goals have been good and clear, such as during the Disruption of 1843. At that time, some 451 ministers walked out of the established church in protest. In almost every case it was at enormous personal sacrifice. This newly formed Free Church had only fifty buildings, no stipends and few manses. Yet it is still staggering to reflect that within one year, according to J.H.S. Burleigh, four hundred seventy new buildings had been completed and others were in process of erection, furnished mostly through local resources. We have seen that the present problems of the Kirk are not all of its own making, but it is true that it has lost much respect from the people of this country. Leaders must gain a vision of the future and set realistic and achievable goals appropriate to such a vision. To regain national respect, these must be goals sympathetic to the real problems of the nation, goals which inspire and challenge, and goals which are grounded in the ministry of Jesus. A little tinkering with one verse of the old hymn sums it up:

If with the vision glorious
Her longing eyes were blest,
She'd be the Church victorious
And not the Church at rest

It would in a way be comforting to think that the church might be heading for that kind of public crisis which would dramatically focus minds upon the nature of the problem. It would be good to think that a honest confession "Hey Dad, we shrank the church" would lead to that urgent concentration of thought and skill which could engender a new reformation. However, from where we stand, we cannot see either a public crisis or an honest confession.

The evident widespread concern among ministers and members has to become critical assessment. The development of a long-term strategy is one essential component which is currently missing. If a clear analysis could be presented and the benefits accruing made obvious, members could begin to regain confidence even though sacrifice remained central to the process.

The church should aim to transform the world and its witness should be costly. If that means going out with a bang then so be it. An sudden exodus with integrity beats an endless shrinkage accompanied by a whine and a whimper.

Questions for Discussion

1. Do you discern in the church a clear statement of current problems with a clear vision of how to tackle them?

2. What should be the main component of such a vision?

3. Do you agree with this analysis of the present state and future course of the church? Why or why not? If not, what is your alternative analysis?

4. Reflecting upon our long Christian heritage, which essential features of the church should be carried into the next phase of its life?

PART III

PERSPECTIVES IN FAITH

Chapter 7

"ON A CLEAR DAY........."

The strength of a man's position in the world depends on the degree of adequacy of his perception of reality. The less adequate it is, the more disorientated and hence insecure he is and hence in need of idols to lean on and thus find security. The more adequate he is, the more he can stand on his own feet and have his centre within himself.--Eric Fromm

Our thesis all along has been that faith ought to make us more clear-sighted, not only in relation to the church but also to the world. So from a faith perspective where are we headed? Here is a dream (a real one) to consider

A man is awakened in a house by his daughters, who have been disturbed by a noise. He goes through the timber house with his daughters, checking each room in turn. There is no sign of an intruder, and having only to check the rear porch, they are ready to return to bed. As one of the girls moves towards the porch she squeals and points to the floor. Through a small hole in the floor it is clear that the house is moving. There are rails visible underneath. It becomes clear that the house has been placed on a train. The man and his daughters remain awake, but sense that the house is being repositioned. To their amazement, when they open the door before dawn, everything seems just the same in the neighbourhood. All the neighbouring houses have been moved as well. Everything looks just the same but it all has been moved, and the next morning no one else appears to be aware that everything has been shifted.

Much has been written about change and about the increasing rate of change due to technological advance. Most people are aware of change-at least on that level where day to day life is played out. Videos, mobile phones, and home computers carry an irresistible force. But at another level we are quite unaware of the profound nature of change in the social order and in the world. We speak not merely of technological change, but also of economic and political change We believe that if we can maintain or advance our standard of living even a little, no matter what goes on around us, then everything will be all right. So we attempt to keep our jobs, maintain our families, seek good education for our children, acquire some possessions; the carriage which transports our 'house' appears intact and we feel relatively secure. But the increasing breakdown in community, the growing social violence, the accelerating gap between rich and poor, the expanding problems posed by drug and alcohol abuse: all these things mean that the landscape through which our carriage is moving is suffering massive changes in its features. Such an alteration in the social context of life affects us all: the people we work alongside, the people who make our meals in restaurants and canteens, the people who sit beside our children at school, and the people who represent us in the political realm. The ostrich response is of no value: what we refuse to look at affects us nevertheless. All are affected by the steadily shifting society. It may be argued, of course, that at times the train may be heading in a positive direction. Social change can be good and beneficial. Whether change appears as good or bad, it is clear that no one can opt out; everyone will be affected. What does such change imply for the future of individuals and society? If it were possible to peer into the future from our moving carriage, what would the landscape look like?

Individualism will surely continue to march ahead, implying the further isolation of people. Behaviour will be increasingly driven by 'whim'. People will cease to ask the question 'why' and be driven only by the question 'why not'?[1] The nuclear family, fragile as it already is, will continue to experience 'fallout' in all senses. Children, shorn of much significant contact with parents and any extended family, will be less secure and be even more difficult to control. 'Community' will exist mainly in terms of short-term pressure groups focused on single issues, giving it a fundamentally selfish base. Institutions such as the church, education, and the law will find it more difficult to carry out their functions, lacking the good will and commitment of the populace.

Technology is bound to push the world along at an even faster rate. Individuals will find it difficult to cope emotionally with the pace of change. Insofar as they become the consumers of technological change, they will be related to one another primarily by electronic communication on a world-wide network. Such a network will also provide the basis for a world economy. Aided by such means, consumerism will increase apace, giving more and more power to those who control the flow of communications and manage international corporations. Everyone will be instantly and always in the market-place. Any sense of a tangible local neighbourhood will disappear, along with privacy and personal space for the prized 'individual'.

Focus on the Future

It is, of course, quite impossible to predict with much accuracy the shape of the future, even on the clearest of days. There are too many complicated factors, and much of life is governed by the collision of random forces. After all, even the most learned observers of international politics failed to predict the rapid crumbling of the Communist empire. But if we did try to look into a future determined by some of these forces and factors , what would it look like?

We might well picture the World Individual, connected to the world network but essentially isolated, living either in considerable luxury or in substantial poverty, geared mainly to the present and not to the past, manipulated by commercial and media powers, relatively insecure and unhappy, and shorn of long-term purpose or direction. Is this too pessimistic a view? Many think not. Eric Fromm writes:

Our contemporary Western Society, in spite of its material, intellectual and political progress, is increasingly less conducive to mental health, and tends to undermine the inner security, happiness, reason and the capacity for love in the individual; it tends to turn him into an automaton who pays for his human failure with increasing mental sickness, and with despair hidden under a frantic drive for work and so-called pleasure.[2]

Such a future is possible because, as in the dream, our attention is focused upon our own house or carriage and not upon change and movement. When individuals concentrate only on doing 'their own thing' and institutions concern themselves only with their own existence, then they ignore and weaken that very fabric which makes such freedom possible. Thus the church concentrates on self-preservation and not on the life of the world; the media is inebriated with its own power and insists on its freedom no matter at what cost; the politicians are concerned largely with devising appealing policies which offer re-election, and not with those policies for the long-term; individuals focus mainly on self and seldom on community. Our expectation of a freedom within a stable order does not square with our actions. This was noted by George Gladstone Robertson, a Glasgow physician who for many years practised in the Gorbals area:

It seems to me that we have our values mixed up and have come to equate survival of the individual with the survival of our race when, if carried to extreme, these concepts are utterly incompatible. Our Empire was built on hard work, thrift and love of risk and adventure. Now that we cannot be bothered with empires we seek pleasant sensations in toys, leisure and sex.[3]

From the perspective of faith, such a view of the future is sufficiently bleak to horrify, to represent a denial of our nature as human beings and signify a step backward for the world. The Christian view is that we are social beings and require to be social beings. This means that relationships are essential for the growth and maturing of individuals. Only in the mutual transactions of people, in their caring, forgiving, and working together is the development of an authentic human spirit possible. Moreover, we believe that the community called together to be encouraged and challenged by the Word of God is a key place for such transactions. Our conversation with God requires our conversation with one another: if any one says they love God but hate their brothers and sisters, they are lying. So social justice is also an essential component of the larger community. The values required for a being to become fully human cannot be adequately known, transmitted and internalised without commitment to this kind of life together. It is certain that in the lively community of faith that such values are recalled, appreciated and passed on. Community provides the context for persons to gain a sense of purpose, security, happiness, and physical and mental well-being. If from our moving carriage we cannot see and attend to an inclusive community, then our final destination may be either chaos or destruction. Faith, hope and love are the necessary ingredients for the creation of this essential type and quality of community.

Questions for Discussion

1. List the most important technological and social changes you have seen in your lifetime. Try to spell out as specifically as possible how these have affected institutions and individuals.

2. What is the long-term effect of individualism on relationships likely to be, particularly between adults and children?

3. Where in your own life have you experienced the greatest sense of community?

4. Exactly how do faith, hope and love operate in the creation of community at the local, national, and international level?

Chapter 8

"AN ALTERNATIVE VISTA"

...the church does not exist to pat the world on the back; it exists in part at least to do the opposite, to call the world to a fresh start.--Robert McAfee Brown

We consider two relationships in this chapter: the relationship of the church to the world and the relationship of the church to its own history, calling and purpose. These are not separate but inseparably linked. We consider first the church's relationship with the world. The Christian Church does not have to dig very deeply to rediscover its true relationship with the world. Through its long history church leaders have expressed it again and again. John Robinson was one, arguing that "...it is not difficult to recognise the authentic Christian attitude when we see it. The trouble is that we so seldom see it."[1] Robinson outlines a paradoxical combination of concern and detachment: the church is to care more for the world as the creation of God and yet maintain a detachment from many of its fashions and values. It is to lose itself for God *in* the world without losing its heart *to* the world. It is quite clear that living in this tension can never be comfortable; it is painful to attempt and demanding to sustain. For the church to observe a social problem, then offer a solution and try to implement it, only to find its work rejected by individuals and other organisations, can be hard to bear. Such stifling of a positive development leads to feelings of impotence, rejection, and powerlessness among concerned church members. The church faces a persistent battle to avoid the fatigue of failure, to continue to face the issues, to stand up again and again to be counted on the injustices prevalent in every society.

The temptation for the church is to reduce the tension. It is tempting to avoid following the Martin Luther Kings, the George MacLeods, the Trevor Huddlestons and the Desmond Tutus, to change course, pull away, switch off. The temptation is to stay on the sidelines, where the church's best thinking can be employed to discover how many angels can dance on the head of a pin or to solve vexing questions about its own finance and organisation. To be fair, the church has performed well in its pastoral role of supporting organisations who do challenge society more directly, about such issues as the third world, nuclear disarmament and homelessness. Indeed, the church and its membership has contributed massive support for many essential voluntary bodies, finding itself more at ease in the paramedic rather than the storm trooper role.

So the temptation for the church in every era is to live relatively comfortably within the society without calling it to a fresh start. The role of challenging, of shaking the foundations is a constant theme in the Biblical witness. The prophets were called to expose and condemn social injustice; Christ confronted those who exploited ordinary men and women. Moneychangers and Pharisees were left in no doubt about the nature of their abuses. The difficulties involved in overcoming this temptation are immense. We should be under no illusions about how hard it is to recover and maintain the church's prophetic role, uniting vision and will. Eric Fromm suggests that the central task of man is to be fully born. Should the church have a lesser objective? Being fully born must surely mean leaving the comfort of the womb, leaving the known for the unknown, certainty for uncertainty. It will be painful but essential, for remaining in the womb means that there is no view.

If the church as an institution can begin to emerge from its tomb-like existence and begin to fulfil its prophetic role, then the centre of its concern must be for the people of the world who are most vulnerable: the unheard and unnoticed, the unemployed and homeless, the victims of violence and prejudice, the isolated and alienated. It would be a good sign of the birth process if concern for these people occupied us more than our ecclesiastical future. It would be an even better sign if our church took its shape in response to the reality of the present world, rather than to some patterns formed in the last two centuries. Henri Nouwen put it is this disturbing way: "You are only a Christian as long as you pose critical questions to the society you live in..." [2]

We turn now to the question of the church's relationship to its own history, calling and purpose in the world. It will come to no surprise to the reader to discover that we believe the key is community, and the church as one agent creating the necessary quality of community. It is a fundamental misunderstanding to think of the church as the building, or as linked to the minister or as tied to the time of worship. The term 'churchgoer', often used in this country, is a misnomer. People do not *go* to church; they *are* the church as they gather in worship and service. The locus of the love of God is the community of Christians who assemble to hear the Word and enjoy the sacraments. The people are the channels of the love of God as they love, care for, and forgive one another.

So the goal is community, that lively community where an adequate vision of God and the world is shared and renewed week by week. 'Community' is a much used concept and can be understood in numerous ways. A true story will serve to illustrate our particular understanding. A young couple visited a small congregation of some two hundred members in a large Glasgow housing scheme. They attended, with a view to being married there. The young man had largely given up on the church, believing that most people went to show off their new clothes or to catch up on gossip rather than participate in an important act of worship on Sunday morning. But immediately the warmth and diversity of attenders surprised these newcomers. Worship services were actually interesting, with relevant issues being confronted in prayer, talks and music.

Most surprising of all, this tiny congregation, rather than being frightened of or frozen by the massive population surrounding it, strove to meet the many and varied needs of the parish. Whenever the area needed a swimming pool or another sports facility, a shopping centre or community newspaper, the congregation became involved. Sometimes it initiated the campaign. It was hard work but impressive to witness, for clearly the congregation was acting as the hub and heart for the parish. This was not an exclusive elite, but agents of community working alongside Communists, Catholics, atheists and anyone else who wanted to improve the lot of the residents. Old, young, the sports-mad child, the culture vulture, the single parent, the shopper and the swimmer: all were assisted, even though few saw or appreciated the congregation's work.

The couple wishing only to be married slowly began to recognise the importance of this process. Only after a number of years did they appreciate that this was precisely what the church was supposed to do: encourage community for the benefit of all. The God of Christianity is not a solo God, but a three-in-one God: Father, Son and Holy Spirit, a community bound together in love.

The central and thorny question is then: what arrangements best encourage the development of Christian community? In all discussions about the organisation of the church, that question must be the central and controlling one. In this matter, leadership and structures are not neutral. Leaders may either encourage or discourage community; buildings and spaces may either encourage or discourage community.

In the Church of Scotland, as in most churches, it is leadership and buildings which represent the largest outlays in terms of expenditure. In Scotland it is true that there are too many ecclesiastical buildings. Some are in the wrong location due to population movement; some are well-designed and suit the purpose; some depress the spirit and discourage any sense of togetherness; and almost all are expensive to maintain and repair. It is also true that by the church's organisational set-up, it is impossible to make strategic decisions about buildings as a whole. Decisions can only be made when a church is vacant (without a minister!) or in need of major repairs. In this sense, buildings operate as millstones around the church's neck. The common preoccupation at all levels in the church becomes the care and maintenance of buildings rather than living the gospel in the world. This attitude must be changed , and quickly.

The problem of buildings is tied in part to the problem of (professional) ministers. There is insufficient flexibility about the way that ministries are exercised in the church. At the moment ministers are able to stay in their post until retirement, which means in turn that unsuitable buildings must also be retained. Strategic decisions about any particular area is difficult because of this feature. If ministers were on short-term, renewable, contracts, then such decisions could be made much more readily. People with special skills could be matched with congregations having similar needs. Styles or patterns of worship suitable for certain areas of the country could be developed. Team ministries could be put into place where required. It might well be that some congregations could manage (even flourish?) without the regular leadership of an ordained person.

In such a scenario, new training would be required. New skills in teamwork, supervision and managing would need to be acquired. The genuine enabling of members to take on ministry is vital. This is a particularly attractive proposition, for it would encourage all members (the laity) to participate, thus breaking the myth which identifies the church with the minister. It would permit more members to exercise and thus develop their gifts within the worshipping community. Participation by the laity leads directly to increased involvement and responsibility. If the laity are not encouraged and equipped for that ministry within the community how can they be expected to carry their faith to factory floor or office or meal table? It is there that they represent Christ. For ordained ministers, part-time work in schools, hospitals and offices would supplement a part-stipend or salary and help to 'ground' the worship they lead .

Clearly, such changes would mean a tremendous shift in status for ministers, especially in respect of their tenure of appointment. Most ministers are committed, conscientious and hard-working. Their skills, especially in the area of pastoral care, are exercised effectively in times of crisis and need. This occurs without great fanfare and often without much genuine recognition of what has been done. Yet ministers are also much influenced by the expectations of others (congregational members, the church hierarchy and social trends), all of which foster a conservatism regarding their role. This often means that they are defensive or protective about their ministry, rather than sharing it with others. Such a change would be highly controversial, and would need the approval of the majority of ministers. For this purpose much courage would be required to break our bondage to the past.

Model Making

For the sake of discussion, it is possible to propose two contrasting models of the church in the future: the 'Supermarket Model' and the 'Corner shop Model'. Current thinking in the church appears to be most akin to the Supermarket model. In response to the shrinking of resources, one central church building and congregation would displace a number of churches in a given area. In a larger building, with a larger congregation and more resources, a professional staff could be engaged. Teams comprised perhaps by ministers specialising in preaching, pastoral care, and education could be organised, as is the case in the United States of America. This concentration of resources in terms of both money, manpower and lay leadership could make for a livelier and more viable congregations.

The supermarket model would also pose certain problems. The distance to the church building from the outer periphery of the area would be greater, discouraging attendance. The functioning of a more professional staff might well discourage rather than promote lay participation. Moreover, there is little evidence to support the idea that people who actually commit themselves to the new congregation. Past experience with church unions would suggest that many members would disappear without trace. Another problem is the emergence under this model of a new kind of monasticism. That is, a large, well-staffed, lively, and 'successful' church always carries the danger of becoming a refuge from the world. Community is created in the church domain, but, sadly, not in the world.

The corner shop model represents the opposite pole. Congregations would be small, meeting in whatever local accommodation is available. Resources would not permit the appointment of a full-time minister, so a part-time person would be responsible for leading worship and organising pastoral care, etc. In such a congregation the development of lay leadership would be essential, requiring the expansion of current schemes and the development of more local training schemes. Hopefully, the community of the 'church' would extend into the wider neighbourhood, creating community there as well. Doctrinal changes would also be required to permit lay people to preach and administer the sacraments. Such a model also has its problems. Accommodation for the congregation on a regular basis might well be tenuous, and certainly would not be as aesthetically pleasing. Undoubtedly, problems of order and good theology would raise their heads, requiring an adequate scheme of supervision by the presbytery. At the same time, the involvement and growth of lay Christians would be encouraged.

It will be obvious that such models of the church in the future are too simplistic. Across Scotland and across any national church there is a wide and diverse range of congregations. No one model could be adequate. Yet to pose such models is at least to offer the starting point for a debate or discussion about the future of the church, for the real issues of professional or lay, full-time or part-time, central or local, big or small are clearly drawn. Our own preference is for the corner shop model, for it encourages rather than inhibits the participation of all members. We shall attempt now to specify how such a church might be organised.

Organising the Corner Shop

Some of the leadership in the congregation will come from ordained, but part-time ministers. In the following we shall use the term 'minister' to refer to a salaried person. This term is used in preference to 'clergy' which is undesirable; however, it should be understood that in its best sense the 'ministry' is that work which is carried out by all. Clearly a radical departure from the traditional training of ministers is called for in the corner shop church. It might prove helpful to consider in a rational way what this might mean.

While our argument has suggested that every member will have a ministry sharing his or her gifts and talents in appropriate ways, we will still require men and women to be ministers of 'Word and Sacrament'. The question is: how are these ministers to be equipped? A possible model for this exercise could be loosely based on Dreyfus' skills acquisition design, which is also used by other professions. It is a development model bringing theory and practical training closer together and would commence at the end of academic training. Under this scheme, ministers would progress through five stages. 'Beginner' ministers would be 'licensed', having limited experience of the situations in which they would be expected to perform. 'Advanced Beginners' have sufficient experience to begin to note the recurring components of situations. The 'Competent' minister has two to three years experience and can begin to see his actions in terms of long-range goals. The 'Proficient' minister has sufficient experience to recognise the typical events to be expected in a given situation. He or she is able to focus quickly on the vital aspects of the problem. The 'Expert' minister would be regarded as the person who, using a wealth of experience, hones in on the accurate region of any problem without wasteful consideration of a large range of unfruitful, alternative solutions. He/she has that intuitive grasp of a situation which permits the formulation of the appropriate action. That is, the expert avoids all attempts to reinvent the wheel. It may be of equal importance for the development of the minister to require a period of living and working together in a residential setting as an essential part of their training.

The church is a living and complex organisation which has many of the dynamics of other human organisations. As such it needs to be studied and dealt with carefully. Currently, too many ministers arrive in parishes straight from college (yes, we include ourselves), having little grasp of such dynamics. They believe themselves to be experts but receive little encouragement from the system to develop their gifts and strategies, a pattern which reinforces their flawed understanding. Congregations may either also reinforce this flawed concept or destroy it (and them) altogether. The reality is more like giving a learner swimmer fours years of instruction on the theory of swimming: every stroke, every situation including lifesaving being covered in minute detail, and then letting him see water for the first time as you push him off the end of the pier on a stormy day.

Clearly the Drefus model for acquiring skills is an ideal and abstract one. The church is fortunate to have many ministers who are indeed experts, but that may be by fortune and chance rather than by design. This model links theory and practice in a very close way and closes the gap between these components in the current regime. It would operate on a fairly long term basis, perhaps ten years. Such a pattern of training would encourage ministers to continue to develop even after the probationary period has been completed, to reflect regularly on practical experience gained from real situations, and reassess their theories of ministry in the light of the above.

Taking the Laity Off the Shelf

The church of the future will depend in equal measure upon adequately trained laity. Of first importance will be a proper understanding of the church and its role in the world. But it is crucial that the training of the laity focus upon teamwork in the ministry of the church. While we do have many 'teams' in the church, do they actually work together collaboratively? All too often they merely demonstrate that in this field the church still has much to learn. Unfortunately, the church at both local and national level, is not very efficient, nor is it much of a team.

There needs to be 'team consciousness' in the church. At the moment congregational leaders exhibit little consciousness of being a part of either a local or a larger team, operating independently for the most part. Moreover, teams are often not formed on a rational basis. Team members are chosen not for their particular skills or personal characteristics, but because they are available. A more rational planning of teamwork would stress that to be effective any team requires to be chosen carefully. Flexibility and ability to adapt to new challenges are essential. Teams come in different shapes and sizes; they consist essentially of a group of variously talented people who make contributions towards the achievement of one common goal. Team building can only happen if the leader is genuinely committed to creating a team. Only after establishing its common thinking on a range of issues can the team expect to promote these through its actions, for effective teamwork is based on shared values. A team's effectiveness can be assessed by the ability to achieve its aim in the most efficient way.

It is doubtful that the church could ever reach complete agreement about its aims, but it could certainly be much more effective in reaching some agreed targets if teamwork were rationally considered. While Kirk Sessions are often referred to as 'teams', they usually do not operate as such. All too often the minister refuses to give elders the autonomy to take decisions without referring to him or to the whole Kirk Session. The constant reference to the 'higher' authority tends to paralyse team working. When authority is properly delegated it inspires confidence and encourages creativity. It is also worth noting that status distinctions within a group tend to reduce interaction and social support among members. The church at all levels is a complex organisation, but through a focus on goals, tasks, roles and procedures, a solid basis for trust and co-operative teamwork can be developed.

There are certain types of skills or roles required within each team to enable it to produce its best work. We have caricatured three of these roles:

The 'Paul' Role-- Highly strung, outgoing and dominant. This person is the task leader, demonstrating a drive to complete the task. He or she may be irritable and impatient, but gets things done.

The 'Isaiah' Role-- Intelligent and analytical, seeing things as they are and as they ought to be. He or she offers creative and challenging ideas.

The 'Joanna' Role-- Supportive, cautious, and good listener. She or he is likeable and popular, but often remains unnoticed when present. The team does not operate well when this person is absent.

All these roles may be filled by males or females. They are capable of being developed much further, but the essence is of three vital types: the task oriented, the creative, and the cautious. Each role requires the others and an effective team cannot be formed without all three. All teams must develop a set of standards concerning correct team behaviour and working practices; they also require structure to function efficiently. The team leader (not necessarily the minister) is a key person requiring a clear vision of the aims of the task and the ability to communicate this to the rest of the group. Being able to move from one leadership style to another is crucial, as is motivating and inspiring team members while maintaining high standards of personal performance. This person must encourage mutual respect and good working relationships even when some attitudes and beliefs are not shared.

Such leadership skills among both the ministry and the laity will be required in the church of the future. In a congregational setting every person must be valued and encouraged to participate. The talent and resources available in the congregation, plus its potential problems must be taken seriously. Thus all team members are invited to seek out deficiencies in the congregation and to suggest possible responses. All defensiveness, resistance to change, buck passing and scapegoating is discouraged.

Christians in the future must see themselves as the church in order for it to be alive and vital and in order to harness all those personal resources which exist in latent form. The organisational form of the church is a matter of great importance, and there will be other models to be considered. But however the church is organised in the future, whether as supermarket or corner shop or other, whether with full-time or part-time ministers, regardless of the buildings- unless this particular problem is solved how can the church be true to its vision of itself? And most importantly, how can it to call the world to a fresh start?

Questions for Discussion

1. Consider any new ways in which the church at both local and national levels could try to influence a complex technological society.

2. Discuss the supermarket and corner shop models of the church. What advantages and disadvantages can you specify about each model?

3. What are the implications of congregations developing without a full-time ordained minister?

4. Would you say that God is blessing or cursing the church at the present, and upon what factors do you base your conclusion?

Chapter 9

FULL ON THE EYE

So what is vision? It is an act of seeing, of course, an imaginative perception of things, combining insight and foresight.-- John Stott

We have been trying to say in this book that many people, both ordinary folk and political leaders, appear to be blind to the dangers towards which the world is moving. Lulled into a sense of security by the relatively intact appearance of their locale (railway carriage), they are blind to the pace and direction of change in the larger society (train). There is a persistent reluctance to look at where the tracks are heading. The change is not merely brought about by our developing technology, but also by the values implicit in the policies which we ourselves have espoused. The social order is unravelling, the world is being homogenised, and life is increasingly dominated by commerce and the media. Individuals are concerned mainly with achieving their own ends and are little concerned with the good of the wider community or society.

In all of the things thus said we are aware that there could be much qualification. Of course individualism is not this simple; of course an emphasis on individual rights has certain benefits; of course technology opens up a fascinating new world, and so on. The trouble is that the endless qualification required for perfect analytical accuracy comes only at the expense of severing the nerve and the springs for action. Our intention in this work is to isolate and identify some of those submerged observations about the church and the world made by us and many others. The point is not to construct a tidy analysis but to initiate that kind of debate which might result in positive change.

We have also said that the church does have a vision of and for the world which could help to correct our blindness and direct us away from the pit. Unfortunately that vision is not operative, for the church has become marginalised and is too preoccupied with its inner life and structures. We have gone on to argue that the church ought to emerge from the relative comfort of its womb to recall its own vision of the world and to share it. So there is a new and profound sense in which the church needs to be *in* the world. Emerging from the womb, it needs to see the world as it is rather than though some ecclesiastically dated or theologically tinted lens. It is a denial both of the doctrines of creation and the incarnation to regard people primarily as souls to be won onto membership rolls. A theology which takes the incarnation seriously will recall that Jesus enjoyed the company of sinners, full stop. He enjoyed sitting long at table with them. The church needs to recover its understanding of the genuine goodness of the creation. So those changed patterns of life noted earlier, neither good nor bad but simply different, need to be recognised and taken on board by the church. All of this is necessary so that the church can adjust its institutional shape in order to proclaim the gospel over against the actual needs of the world. This does not imply an acceptance of the fashions of the age, but simply that kind of intelligent and sacrificial presence in the world that engenders respect. The New Testament metaphors which portray the church as yeast or salt or as an earthen vessel for eating and drinking are important in this respect. They convey the central idea of the church channelling the power and love of God to the world even as the church itself is lost, transformed or broken for the sake of the world. The last model- being broken for the sake of the world- seems relevant both to the pattern of Jesus' life, death, and resurrection, and to the current situation. Is the church willing to allow itself to be cracked, splintered and destroyed if in this process it brings new life to the world?

Re-creating Community

The pressing need is for that shared and mutual life where individuals give of themselves for the sake of the whole. In this kind of shared life people are able to risk themselves and thus mature, while learning simultaneously that they are not more important than the whole community. It is in mutual encounters, discussions and projects that they are tested and encouraged to grow, learning to respect the opinions of others, however different. It is through this process that those values and virtues that characterise a civilised and humane society are internalised.

Community is a prerequisite for the full development of valued and unique individuals.

Thus it seems to us that community in our age must to some degree be an act of will. People must willingly give up some of their 'freedom' in order to discover the importance of life together. Time, energy and commitment will need to be given to institutions such as the family, the church and education. This will hardly prove to be popular, so fiercely do people cling to the fashion of individual freedom. Yet the gains to be made in terms of personal growth and meaning are enormous. Social stability can be gained, a result of helping young people to move through that 'no man's land' between childhood and adulthood. Personal security can be gained, a result of knowledge that one is meaningfully related to others and from the social integration of those with learning difficulties or physical handicaps.

It also seems to us that people will need to resist some of the enormous pressures applied to them. The homogenisation of the world through the electronic media must be resisted. Differences between cultures and faiths and traditions will need to be valued, respected and protected. It will be even more difficult to resist employing the yardstick of money as the key measure of life. We must be shifted from our conception of self as consumer and from preoccupation with our 'personal rights'. This may sound like unparalleled idealism, yet without idealism there can be no vision. Without vision there is no other possibility for the future. Indeed, without vision the people perish.

The world as *one* community has to be the final aim for the Christian. The Christian faith insists that the love of Christ is the norm for human existence, a love which should be expressed through our responsibility for the welfare of other people. One great thinker called this the 'ultimate social problem of human history'.[1]

It is hardly possible, however, to talk about a world community until there is some re-creation of local community. Building community, as in other great enterprises, is a gradual work- the laborious laying of brick after brick. When people give themselves to this work they will discover a number of benefits. A deeper knowledge of self and of others, and the development of previously unknown skills are important aspects of the building process. As targets are set and achieved, confidence grows, and the value of the whole group begins to be recognised. Faith, trust, confidence and hope will be rediscovered as interdependent features of community life. A developing richness and depth to relationships help to overcome inevitable disagreements. The crucial question is: how and where does the work of building community begin?

The Church as A Model

We believe that there are grounds for hope in that we know that the church could provide one model for this kind of community. It has in the past and still does so in many areas of the world. Even in Britain and in Scotland, there are congregations which show those marks of an authentic community . They are not greatly encouraged by the larger denominational structure; nor do they receive much beneficial publicity, but they do function. Men and women, rich and poor, fit and ailing, young and old, gather to worship regularly, and their worship affects their view of the world, their work and their leisure; they accept responsibility for the ongoing life of the wider community and give generously of their time, talents and money. In their fellowship, love, mutual acceptance, encouragement, and forgiveness can be experienced. The door is open to all: the poor, the handicapped, the homeless and unemployed. How might the faith and life of such a church community be continued and better expressed in the future?

Faith could be understood as a life-long 'conversation' with God. Such a conversation is a daily event, involving thanksgiving for life, the celebration of what God has done in the past and is doing in the present, questions about the meaning and purpose of life, all of this conducted in a language that is ordinary but respectful. God is not much impressed by flowery flattery or by the endless repetition of pious phrases. Too much language in worship treats God as either excessively vain or extremely foolish. While such a conversation includes expressions of loyalty and love, it may also include expressions of anxiety, doubt and anger. This kind of conversation is not entirely verbal in its content. The use of silence, movement, colour and song should also be present and helps to build up our relationship with the source of life. The willingness to have such a conversation over a lifetime and the brave refusal to end it constitute faith.

We believe that this kind of conversation with God has its focus in Jesus of Nazareth. Jesus reveals both the divine nature and the human nature to us. The 'otherness' of God is seen not primarily in the 'religious' or 'miraculous' aspect of Jesus' life but in the quality of his humanity. In Jesus, God is found to be 'with us'. This awareness permits the discovery of our true nature and spurs our growth to maturity, and so represents an answer to the persistent question 'Who am I?' It also permits the admission of our failings and shortcomings and prepares us for the next stage of our journey.

Furthermore, we believe that the locus of the love of God is that community which gathers to hear and to speak the Word of God, celebrate the sacraments, and enjoy fellowship one with another. Only in such a community is it possible for people to gain that genuine freedom which permits them to take the risk of learning together, sharing their concerns, and discovering the value of forgiveness. In that community the Spirit is present to kindle hope, mutual understanding, growth in the faith, and love both for the neighbour and enemy.

In all of this we believe that the resurrection must be central, however it is interpreted. The resurrection of Jesus, rather than his crucifixion and death, is at the centre of the faith. An unbalanced emphasis on the death of Christ by the church has resulted in the continual reinforcement of those patterns and mind-sets associated with death. Thus the church itself has made an unintentional theological contribution to its own decline. It is crucial for the church to understand that the resurrection should be the central reality and motivating factor in its life. The continuing 'rebirth' of the church in the world is not an option but rather a demand made clear and possible by the resurrection of Jesus.

The church as community is not a new idea but one which is central to the New Testament. The church is understood in organic terms as the Body of Christ, and all believers are members of that body. Each part of the body needs the others and each one has something to contribute to the health and functioning of the whole. Hence, as we have already said, the church of the future must develop a much better way of recognising and employing the gifts of all its members. Their abilities and interests must be quite deliberately recognised, encouraged and channelled, not merely to permit their own growth in the faith but also to further the growth of the whole body. In New Testament terms, every part of the body is important. No part of the body should be ignored or taken for granted.

The importance of recognising and valuing each person in the church can hardly be stressed too much, for this is a radical departure from the way things have been in the past. An example will demonstrate why this is so. Elsie (a real person) was a committed church member to the end of her days, giving generously of her time, talents and money. She attended worship every week, supporting the Woman's Guild and enjoying her contacts. She had been an able student at school, and had worked as a personal secretary in a long-established optician's practice, a position of some responsibility. She was clever with her hands, could knit, sew, and embroider. Elsie was a competent artist, had learned how to play a musical instrument and had taken various night classes. Having a cheerful, generous, and caring disposition, she had an immense amount to offer, including time and money. Yet her gifts were never recognised or used to further her congregation nor to help her further explore the Christian faith other than by being a passive recipient. She had a clear notion of how to support the church but was never encouraged to see herself as the church. Far too many Elsies have sat passively in the pews.

The corner shop church is in a better position to use the Elsies. In small congregations with less than three hundred members, every member can be known by the others, for old and young people meet and mix regularly. They can share their hopes and fears in the light of their faith through individual conversations, in groups, or in worship. Members gain insights from the experience of others, and such insights subtly change their attitudes. This in turn improves the quality of their service in the world within the work, leisure and family spheres. Moreover, those small groups in towns and villages made up by members from the immediate area are well-suited by their experience to respond to local issues. Such a congregation can serve as the base community to initiate support or criticism for projects affecting everything from schools to water supply. When the denomination meets in its regional and national grouping it is important to have representation and contributions from a fifteen member island congregation as well as from a fifteen hundred member city congregation. Indeed, a church may only claim to be a national church if it receives input from all geographical areas.

Finally, the church has to attempt to share its vision of the world as God's good creation requiring the attention and care of humanity. If the leaders of nations and people of the world are unable to grasp a sense of direction and purpose, if immediate gain and individual freedom are the only ends embraced, then the future will indeed be bleak. The church must awaken humanity, opening its eyes to its true nature, opening its eyes to the source of all life, and opening its eyes to the responsibility of caring for creation. This is the church's proper prophetic role: opening the eyes of the blind. When seen and perceived, this vision may be startling in its clarity, bestowing the power to re-shape reality. Such a power was recognised by Robert Burns in his poem *The Vision*: [2]

> **And when the bard, or hoary sage,**
> **Charm or instruct the future age,**
> **They bind the wild poetic rage**
> **In energy**
> **Or point the inconclusive page**
> **Full on the eye.**[2]

Questions for Discussion

1. Should the differences between cultures, faiths and traditions be valued and protected? Why, and how can this be done?

2. Imagine an ideal congregation. Does it genuinely value young and old, fit and ailing? Does it include people in the whole life of the church? How does it share its strengths with the wider church?

3. By what process could *all* church members come to understand themselves as the church, the active and living people of God? Would this pose a threat to anyone?

4. Do you believe that the church, armed with its vision, could have the ability to transform reality?

Notes

Chapter 1

1. Margaret Thatcher, *Speaking Personally as a Christian*
2. Peter Berger, *Invitation to Sociology: A Humanistic Perspective* (New York: Doubleday Anchor), p.121.
3. See, for example, Ronald Gregor Smith, *Secular Christianity* (London: Collins, 1966)
4. *The Herald,* November 2, 1993
5. *The Scotsman,* September 23, 1993
6. *The Scotsman,* September 3, 1993
7. *The Scotsman,* May 10, 1994
8. *The Scotsman,* October 9, 1993
9. *Financial Times,* September 9, 1993
10. *The Observer,* October 3, 1993

Chapter 2

1. Colin Morris, *God in a Box,* (Hodder and Stoughton), p.11.
2. Colin Morris, "The Theology of the Nine O'Clock News", *Religion and The Media,* Chris Arthur (ed.) (Cardiff: University of Wales Press, 1993), p.138.
3. Michael Novak, *Television as a Social Force* (New York: Praeger, 1975), p.9.
4. South American TV Programme
5. Brian Keenan, *An Evil Cradling,* (Vintage, 1992), p.133.

Chapter 3

1. Joyce McMillan, *Scotland on Sunday*, March 20. 1994.
2. Paul Oestreicher, *The Double Cross*, (Darton, Longman and Todd, 1986), p.89.
3. *The Herald*, March 29, 1994.

Chapter 4

1. Mark Gibbs and T. Ralph Morton, *God's Lively People* (London: Fontana, 1971), p.209.
2. See for example James Gustafson, *Treasure in Earthen Vessels* (New York: Harper & Row, 1961)
3. Martin Luther King, *Letter from the Birmingham Jail*

Chapter 5

1. D. Allan Easton, *Now is the Day*, p.24.

Chapter 6

1. *Reports to the General Assembly*, 1994, p.12.
2. *Reports to the General Assembly*, 1994, p.69.
3. *Reports to the General Assembly*, 1994, p.71.
4. *Reports to the General Assembly*, 1994, p.289.
5. Robert McAfee Brown, *The Significance of the Church* (Philadelphia: The Westminster Press, 1956), p. 87.

Chapter 7

1. Eric Fromm, *The Art of Being* (London: Constable, 1993), p.28.
2. Eric Fromm, *The Art of Being,* p.35.
3. George Gladstone Robertson with Roderick Grant, *Gorbals Doctor,* (London: Jarrolds, 1970), p.186.

Chapter 8

1. John A. T. Robinson *On Being the Church in the World* (London: SCM Press, 1960), p.18.
2. Henri Nouwen, as quoted by Richard Foster, *Money, Sex & Power* (Hodder & Stoughton, 1985), p.247.

Chapter 9

1. Reinhold Neibuhr, *On Politics,* ed. by H.R. Davis and R.C. Good, (New York: Charles Scribner & Sons, 1960), p. 342.
2. Robert Burns, *Burns Poetical Works* (London and Glasgow: Collins), p.150.